The Last Hour
The First Hour
The Forty-Second Generation

A Volume of the Eschatology Series

By Donald A. Peart

Table of Contents

Preface 1

Understanding the Times 3

The Last Hour.. 13

The Overlap 24

Wonderful One.. 33

Seventy Times Seven.. 42

The First Hour 48

The Hour of the Dark Ones 60

The Hour of His Crisis 69

Preface

Jesus has the answers to the many questions which arise about time, and admittedly, the Lord sometimes tells us certain things are none of our business. The disciples asked: "Lord, will You at this time restore the kingdom to Israel?" Jesus' reply: "It is not for you to know times or seasons which the Father has put in His own authority" *(Acts 1:6-7)*.

In this case, relative to the kingdom of Israel, the disciples did not need to know God's timing. There are some set times God will keep from us to protect us. Yet, there are times and seasons into which he will give us a glimpse. "The secret things belong unto the LORD our God: but those things which are revealed belong unto us and to our children forever, that we may do all the words of this law" *(Deuteronomy 29:29)*.

There are certain times and seasons that God reveals unto us. The apostle Paul gave the descriptions of the "last days," Apostle Peter also discussed the "last days." John, the beloved apostle, boldly declared in his day "that it is the last hour." The book of Revelation also unveils the "first hour." My point is this: There are some things concerning "timing" that God has made know to His Church by giving His Church an "understanding of the times." A good example of this is: Paul indicates that the Day of the Lord is like a pregnant woman who has labor pains *(1 Thessalonians 5:1-4)*.

Thus, some of the dynamics of the Day of the Lord, which comes as a thief in the night can be understood by studying the process of childbearing. We can understand the times of God. The Church just has to learn the right way of telling time.

If a child is not trained how to tell the time, he/she may think that the minute hand is the hour hand and vice versa. This is the problem in the Church. We have not been taught how to tell time. We still filter the Scriptures through the wrong traditional teachings from our fathers.

As a preface to the upcoming chapters, I cite Jesus' response to the religious leaders who could not discern how to tell time. They were looking at the fulfillment of prophecy in the "time" realm and could not deduce that the sign (the Wonderful One — Jesus) of their visitation was present. How do we tell time? We tell time by the hour hand and the minute hand of events ("signs"), as outlined by the living God.

Matthew 16:1-3, NKJV: ¹*Then the Pharisees and Sadducees came, and testing Him asked that He would show them a sign from heaven.* ²*He answered and said to them, "When it is evening you say, 'It will be fair weather, for the sky is red';* ³*and in the morning, 'It will be foul weather today, for the sky is red and threatening.' Hypocrites! You know how to discern the face of the sky, but you cannot discern the signs of the times.*

May the understanding of the times (the ability to discern the "signs of the times") be realized as you read this book; and as you spend quality time *with* Jesus!

Blessings,

Donald A. Peart, called to be a son of the Father

Understanding the Times

1 Chronicles 12:32, NKJV: ... Issachar who had understanding of the times, to know what Israel ought to do ....

Jesus understood timing. He did not let people push Him to do things out of season *(John 2:4; John 7:6)*. He knew the "hour" when He would be betrayed *(Matthew 26: 43)*. Jesus knew how long to wait before He raised Lazarus from the dead *(John 11: 1-15)*.

In like manner, "understanding of the times" has been an important aspect of my relationship with our Lord Jesus Christ. It is our God given privilege to know what the Israel of God (the Church) ought to be doing, and to know when to do.

Those who "pay the price," for so "Issachar" means, can understand certain times of God. The only absolute set time that God has hidden from us is the time (hour) of Jesus' physical return (if one looks at *Matthew 24:35-39* beyond the context of Jesus — the destruction of Jerusalem in A.D. 70).

Matthew 24:36, NKJV: But of that day and hour no one knows, not even the angels of heaven, but My Father only.

Mark 13:32, NKJV: But of that day and hour no one knows, not even the angels in heaven, nor the Son, but only the Father ...

In the world in which we live, knowing the time for everything is of utmost importance. We must know what time to go to work. A doctor's office is built around scheduling: the time a patient arrives, how long it should take to see a particular patient (time intervals), etc. If there were no set time to do anything, then when would anything start?

If there were no deadline established for things to come to an end, there would be no new beginning. Jesus used creation,

3

and examples of everyday life to teach spiritual things. Our daily lives are built upon a principle of understanding timing.

We know when to do what we need to do, and we plan accordingly. It is the same way for spiritual things. God has a time for everything under heaven; and we should know the seasons and times of God and plan accordingly.

Ecclesiastes 3:1, NKJV: To everything there is a season, a time for every purpose under heaven …

Therefore, it is not strange to want to know when certain things will happen on the earth relative to God and His Church. There is a time for everything under heaven *(Ecclesiastes 3:1)*. There is a time for the last hour. There is a time for the first hour.

God is so wise that he gave the Church the tool to know time. Mankind has invented timepieces to know and track time. In like manner, one of God's "timepieces" which His Children use to tell time is the tabernacle built by Moses.

Hebrews 9:2; 9, NKJV: [2]For a tabernacle was prepared: the first part, in which was the lampstand, the table, and the showbread, which is called the sanctuary… [9] It was symbolic for the present time in which both gifts and sacrifices are offered which cannot make him who performed the service perfect in regard to the conscience …

The tabernacle of Moses was divided into three parts — the Outer Court, The Holy Place ("the first part"), and The Holy of Holies ("second part" — *Hebrews 9:7)*. The Scripture then referred to time relative to the priestly functions in certain areas of the tabernacle. The practice of animal sacrifices[1] in the holy place was referred to as a "symbol for the present

---

[1] After Jesus abolished sacrifices (Heb. 10:9-10; Dan. 9:27), animal sacrifices continued (Acts 21:26) until they were stopped completely by the destruction of Jerusalem and its temple in A.D. 70.

time" – the "present time" of last days of animal sacrifices and the beginning of the early Church.

Hebrews 9:9a, NIV: "This is an illustration for the present time …."

The tabernacle of Moses, along with its functions, is full of symbolism. One of the aspects of the Tabernacle's symbols is the understanding of time. As indicated above, the tabernacle of Moses was made of three areas: the Outer Court, the Holy Place, and the Holy of Holies.

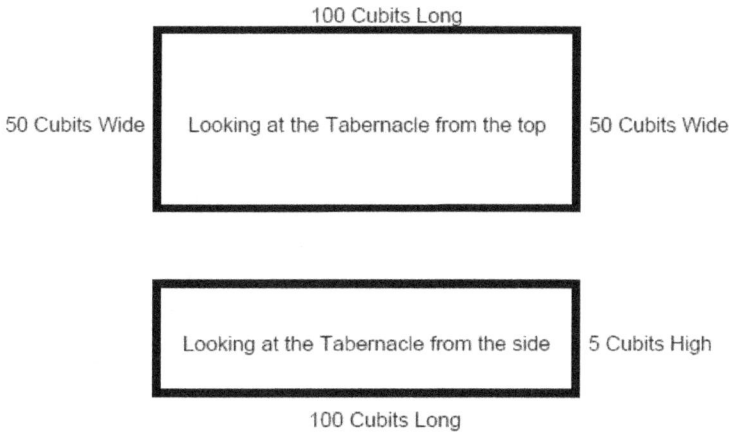

100 Cubits Long

50 Cubits Wide	Looking at the Tabernacle from the top	50 Cubits Wide

Looking at the Tabernacle from the side	5 Cubits High

100 Cubits Long

The dimensions of the Outer Court are as follows: the Outer Court was one hundred (100) cubits long. The width was fifty (50) cubits wide. The height was five (5) cubits high (see sketches below). Note: By looking at the dimensions of the tabernacle from different points of view, we can see different layers of truth. Thus, my point of view is not dogmatic.

Adding all the dimensions (perimeter) of the Outer Court (100 + 100 + 50 + 50 = 300 cubits) and multiplying the total by the height of five cubits (300 cubits x 5 cubits = 1,500 square cubits), the total as indicated is fifteen hundred square cubits. The Law of Moses, including animal sacrifices, lasted approximately fifteen hundred (1,500) years before it was abolished by the sacrifice of Jesus Christ.

Therefore, the writer of Hebrews defined the act of animal sacrifice by its counterparts (the Jews who did not believe in Jesus) as a symbol of the time then present. Even though Jesus' sacrifice did away with all other sacrifices, there was an overlap of time between the sacrifice of Jesus that abolished all other sacrifices, and the continuance of animal sacrifices for a season *(Acts 21:26)*.

Daniel 9:27a, NKJV: Then he [Jesus] shall confirm (lit.; strengthen) a covenant with many for one week; But in the middle of the week, He shall bring an end to sacrifice and offering...

Hebrews 8:6, NKJV: But now He has obtained a more excellent ministry, inasmuch as He is also Mediator of a better (lit.; stronger) covenant, which was established on better promises.

Hebrews 10:8-10, NKJV: ⁸Previously saying, "Sacrifice and offering, burnt offerings, and offerings for sin You did not desire, nor had pleasure in them" (which are offered according to the law), ⁹then He said, "Behold, I have come to do Your will, O God." He takes away the first that He may establish the second.

The age of the law of animal sacrifices (~1,500 years) was ended by Jesus' sacrifice, and the age of the Church was begun through Jesus' crucifixion. It was Jesus who "strengthens a covenant" (the New Covenant) named by Daniel. The proof is found in *Hebrews 8:6* where Jesus is "the Mediator of a better (Gk.; stronger) covenant." The emphasis in the book of Hebrews is the word "stronger" (see Strong's Concordance NT #2909) which coincides with "to be strong" (Strong's Concordance OT # 1396) in *Daniel 9:27.* Jesus' sacrifice also abolished animal sacrifice forever.

"He shall bring an end to sacrifice and offering..." This period (the New Covenant with no more animal sacrifices) for the Church is also depicted by the tabernacle of Moses. Inside the Tent of Meeting were two other sections that comprise the entire tabernacle, the Holy Place, and the Holy of Holies. The Holy Place was ten (10) cubits wide, twenty (20) cubits long, and ten (10) cubits high (see sketches below).

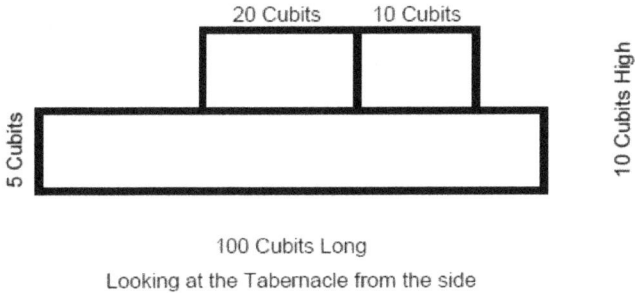

100 Cubits Long
Looking at the Tabernacle from the side

Looking at the Tabernacle from the top

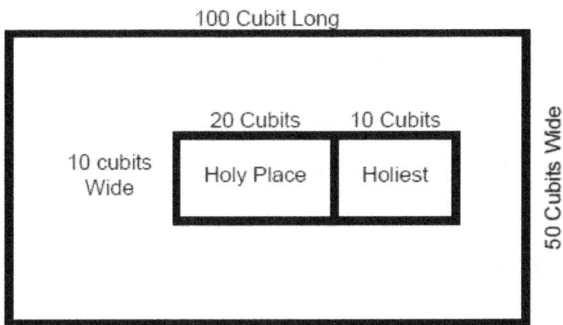

Again, using simple mathematics, 20 x 10 x 10 equals 2,000 cubits. The Holy Place of the Tabernacle of the congregation shows that the Church has been in existence for approximately 2,000 years.[2] The Church age, as we know it,

---

[2] Dr. Kelley Varner, who was a mentor to me for approximately 16 years, who also became as a father to me for approximately 4 years before his passing, pioneered these principles

will only last for approximately[3] 2,000 years. We are coming to the close of the second millennium from Jesus Christ's death, burial, and His powerful resurrection.

The victorious Church is about to recognize the next admeasurements of the tabernacle called the millennium rule. In other words, the dimensions of the Holy Place are symbolic of the present duration of the Church age. It follows that the dimensions of the Holy of Holies along with its furniture(s) provides the pattern of the millennium. To give a little more proof that the numbers harmonize, the Holy of Holies dimensions were 10 Cubits x 10 Cubits x 10 Cubits for a total of 1,000 cubits. The volume of the Holiest of Holies is the same length as the millennium — 1,000 years *(Revelation 20:4-6)*.

Hebrews 10:7 states that "In the volume of the book it is written of Me [Jesus]." The "book" from God that Believers use is the Bible. I believe every answer is in the Bible and can be ascertained by the Spirit of Jesus whenever He is ready to reveal it. The answer to every question is within the Bible. In every seed is a tree. In the Scriptures are the full answers about all Things that are intended to be known about Jesus and His Church.

Hebrews 10:5-7, NKJV: 5Therefore, when He came into the world, He said: "Sacrifice and offering You did not desire, But a body You have prepared for Me. 6In burnt offerings and sacrifices for sin You had no pleasure. 7Then I said, 'Behold, I have come — In the volume of the book it is written of Me — To do Your will, O God.' "

The Greek word translated "of" is "peri." "Peri" is defined as "through (all over)," "around," "circuit," etc. Thus, everything about Jesus is found in the volume of the Bible. In the Bible are God's timetables for every event under the

---

[3] We could add approximately thirty-three years for the lifetime of Jesus before the blood of the New Covenant was in force.

heavens, except for the date when Jesus will come. No one knew and/or knows the day or hour of "the coming of the Son of Man," except for the Father *(see Matthew 24:36-39; Matthew 25:13)*. An idiot (Gk.; "idiotes") attempts to predict the exact day of Jesus' coming.

2 Peter 1:20, NKJV: Knowing this first, that no prophecy of Scripture is of any private (Gk.; idías) interpretation …

In ancient Greek culture, there was a practice to go to the town square and confer on matters with at least two or three persons. An idiot ("idiotes") was one who would not confer with a group but would only confer with himself. "Idotes" is from "idías."

Therefore, no prophecy of Scripture is from an idiot. The prophets conferred with someone—the Father, the Son, and the Holy Spirit. It follows that anyone who "privately" makes predictions about the date of Jesus' exact coming is an idiot.

They are conferring with themselves. How do I know they are idiots? Jesus said the Father has not told anyone, including the Son of God, when He plans for Jesus to come again. Why then do some think they are more special than Jesus for God to tell them something He did not even tell His uniquely begotten?

However, God will allow his apostles and prophets to know "times" (plural) and "seasons" (plural) as demonstrated in *Joel 2:7, 1 Thessalonians 5:1-2 and Ephesians 3:9*. This knowledge can be found in "the volume of the book." In the Book, Peter stated that he knew the signs of the last days (plural). In the volume of the Book, John boldly stated that he knew the last hour which I believe to be approximately the last forty-two years[4] before the destruction of Jerusalem in A.D. 70.

*2 Peter 3:3, NJKV: Knowing this first: that **scoffers** will come in the last days ...*

*1 John 2:18-19, NKJV: Little children, it is the last hour; and as you have heard that the Antichrist is coming, **even now** many antichrists have come, by which we know that it is **the last hour.***

John and Peter declared that they knew the ambient time or times of their period. However, they did not say that they were predicting the day Jesus will return. Even Jesus did not say He knew the exact day.

He stated that His coming would involve "days" — plural *(Luke 17:27)*. In like manner, we also have the privilege of knowing times, seasons, and days; and the tabernacle of Moses is just one of those "timepieces" in the Book. One of the other avenues by which God's timetable is released is by the Holy Spirit — "He [The Spirit] will tell you things to come" *(John 16:13 last part)*.

In the same chapter where John discussed the "last hour," he indicated that because of the "anointing from the Holy One [Jesus]...you know all things" *(I John 2:20)* – not, "some" things, but "all things." The apostle Paul also stated that he had taught the Church the indicators of the "times" (plural) and "seasons" (plural) relative to our Lord coming.

1 Thessalonians 5:1-4, NKJV: ¹But concerning the times and the seasons, brethren, you have no need that I should write to you. ²For you yourselves know perfectly (lit; know exactly) that the day of the

---

[4] Refer to Chapter 6, *The First Hour*, for development of the principle of one hour equaling approximately forty-two years.

Lord so comes as a thief in the night ... ⁴But you, brethren, are not in darkness, so that this Day should overtake you as a thief.

Concerning the day of the Lord, Paul indicated that Jesus would come as a thief. However, Jesus would not come as a thief to His Church that knew times and seasons. Listen to Paul's words: "But you, brethren, are not in darkness, so that this Day should overtake you as a thief." Only those who live "in darkness" cannot see the time of the Day.

We have the ability to "know exactly" the "times" and "seasons." The key to knowing how to tell time by God's "timepiece" is to understand what to look for; one hand on a clock counts by seconds, another counts by minutes and another counts by hours. Jesus calls this the ability to "discern the signs of the time" *(Matthew 16:3)*.

We must know what to look for in order to tell what time His Church are in. In the following chapters, I will show you how to reckon time by the movement of events. Just like a clock/watch changes time by movement of the hands, so likewise, there are certain events that tell the time of the age. The ambient time of every age can be ascertained by the Saints of the Most High who live in that particular period. "…A wise man's heart discerns (lit.; to know by seeing) both time and judgment (lit.; verdict)" *(Ecclesiastes 8:56)*.

What time is it? It is the Day of the Lord. It is the last hour of this age; and there is an overlap (transition period) between the changing ages. I believe the overlap will last approximately three hundred years. I want to iterate that I said "approximately"⁵ three hundred years. I will now develop these findings.

─────────────────────

⁵ God said that Abraham's descendants would be enslaved for four hundred years. At the time when He said it to Abraham, it was an approximate duration; because

For those who have never heard what I am about to say, please consider what I am about to state according to the gospel that the Lord has given to me. Paul preached a gospel that he called "my gospel." Paul's gospel declared Jesus, His resurrection, His Judgeship; and Paul distinguished between "the preaching of Jesus Christ" and "my gospel." Meaning, his gospel is foremost preaching Jesus; however, "the gospel" is broad with Jesus as the Preeminent One. The gospel encompasses the "gospel of the Kingdom," the "gospel of God," "gospel of peace," "the gospel of Christ," "gospel of your salvation," "gospel of the grace of God," "the everlasting gospel," etc.

Galatians 2:2-3, NKJV: *²And I went up [to Jerusalem] by revelation and communicated to them that gospel which I preach among the Gentiles, but privately to those who were of reputation, lest by any means I might run, or had run, in vain.*

2 Timothy 2:7-8, NKJV: *⁷Consider what I say, and may the Lord give you understanding in all things. ⁸ Remember that Jesus Christ, of the seed of David, was raised from the dead according to my gospel ...*

Romans 2:16, NKJV: *...God will judge the secrets of men by Jesus Christ, according to my gospel.*

Romans 16:25-27, NKJV: *²⁵Now to Him who is able to establish you according to my gospel and the preaching of Jesus Christ, according to the revelation of the mystery... made manifest, and by the prophetic Scriptures has been made known to all nations, according to the commandment of the everlasting God, for obedience to the faith-- ²⁷to God, alone wise, be glory through Jesus Christ forever. Amen.*

---

the captivity lasted for an additional thirty years (Genesis 15:30; Exodus 12:41; Galatians 3:17). Thus, we have to be flexible with God's sovereign timing.

The Last Hour

1 John 2:18, NKJV: Little children, it is the last hour; and as you have heard that the Antichrist is coming, **even now many antichrists have come, by which we know that it is the last hour.**

Jesus gave the apostle John, the disciple whom Jesus loved many insights. It was this John who made a bold statement. He indicated that "it is the last hour." This statement generates many questions. First, if it was the last hour approximately 2,000 years ago, the end as most in the Church think of "the end" should have already happened.

The truth is John was speaking of the last hour of the time in which he lived relative to God's year day principle ("one day is as a thousand years") which will be developed in a subsequent chapter. I am aware that scholars date John's epistles ranging from A.D. 68 to A.D. 98. However, in light of Matthew 24, I believe the last hour that John referenced is the last hour (40-42 years) before the destruction of Jerusalem in A.D. 70.

Secondly, and most importantly, what was John's measure for saying it was the "last hour." At work, we can look at the clock, and tell it is the last hour before the workday ends. In like manner John had a gauge.

This was John's gauge: "The Antichrist is coming," and "even now many antichrists have come, by which we know that it is the last hour." I might add: the "many antichrists" are still the hour-hand of our day to ascertain the ambient time. To fully appreciate the hour-hand of John's clock, let us first discover who "the Antichrist" and the "antichrists" really are, and then expound some more on the last hour of these days.

The "antichrists" are former Believers who used to follow Jesus, and then left Him and His Church *(compare 2 Timothy 4:10)*. The Antichrist is a "spirit" which energizes false prophets, as we will see in a moment. If this understanding can be reached, each person will be able to the see the hour hand of the last hour.

1 John 2:18-19, NKJV: ¹⁸Little children, it is the last hour; and as you have heard that the Antichrist is coming, even now many antichrists have come, by which we know that it is the last hour. ¹⁹They went out from us, but they were not of us; for if they had been of us, they would have continued with us; but they went out that they might be made manifest, that none of them were of us.

The "they" of Verse 19 are the "many antichrists" who "went out" from "us" [the Church]. These antichrists actually left from the Church. They may have been fakes – "none of them were of us." Yet they still went out from "us" — the true Believers. Do you see this? In other words, a Christ-like-one can gauge the last hour by the fact that so called anti-Christians are falling away from the faith. Let me explain this a little more.

There are Churches filled with antichrists. "Antichrist" in the Greek means, in place of Christ, or instead of Christ. Many Churches have replaced the true Jesus Christ with their man-made-antichrist. Look at most of the Church world today. Abominable images of men and money are the antichrists they are projecting as God's image.

They went out from the true Church with another image, the image of antichrist. In the stead of Jesus Christ, they have set up another-christ. The antichrists are also those who have become anti-Christians, because of their experiences with the antichrists who are posing as true Christ-like-ones.

In other words, many people are refusing to fellowship in a Church atmosphere, because they have had a bad experience with fake Christ-like ones. They want God without His Church. Yet, one cannot separate Jesus and His Church. Jesus and His Church is one Body. The attitude of wanting God without His Church is an antichrist attitude. A person cannot say he/she walks with Jesus and not fellowship with His Church *(Hebrews 10:25)* [Even though, there may be one (1) true preacher to every eight hundred and fifty (850) persons who call themselves ministers of the gospel — *see 1 Kings 18:19-22* — God is still requiring fellowship with the true Believers].

There are strong possibilities sincere people are being led by false prophets — antichrists. Do not let the false prophets of Baal (Satan) and Asherah (spirits of antichrist) deter you from fellowshipping with the Lamb of God and His Church. There are ministers of the Truth who really exist today. They may be one in a thousand *(Ecclesiastes 7:28b; 1 Kings 18:19)*; but, God always has a remnant of true Ministers and Christians *(Romans 11:3-4 with 1 Kings 19:10; 19:14; 19:18).*

The other examples of antichrists are those who once believed, and then crucify Jesus again by going back into the world *(Hebrews 6).* John echoed the same idea: "[18] … many antichrists have come, by which we know that it is the last hour. [19]They went out from us…" The Scriptures teach that partaking of certain things of God, and then turning your back on Him constitutes crucifying Jesus, again.

Hebrews 6:4-6, NKJV: [4]For it is impossible for those who were once enlightened, and have tasted the heavenly gift, and have become partakers of the Holy Spirit, [5]and have tasted the good word of God and the powers of the age to come, [6]if they fall away, to renew them again to repentance, since they crucify again for themselves the Son of God and put Him to an open shame.

15

There are a lot of people (antichrists) who fell from following the true examples of Jesus. In the process, they have crucified him again. This truth is a sign of the time. The last hour is upon us. Some people are putting Jesus "to an open shame" by revolting against things of God they have shared in experientially

The "Antichrist" (singular) is also another aspect by which we can tell it is the last hour. First, one must understand that the "Antichrist" is not "the beast" as we have heard. Antichrist is a beast *(Revelation 13:11)*; however, the antichrist is not "the first beast" *(Revelation 13: 10-11)*, as we have been taught. The antichrist is "another beast" or "the false prophet" as the book of Revelation calls it *(Revelation 13:11; Revelation 16:13)*. The antichrist is the "spirit" of the "many false prophets" which is "another beast" in addition to "first the beast."

*1 John 4:1-3, NKJV:,*¹*Beloved, do not believe every spirit, but test the spirits, whether they are of God, because many false prophets have gone out into the world.* ²*By this you know the Spirit of God: Every spirit that confesses that Jesus Christ has come in the flesh is of God,* ³*and every spirit that does not confess that Jesus Christ has come in the flesh is not of God. And this is the spirit of the Antichrist, which you have heard was coming, and is now already in the world.*

For some of you reading this material, you may be saying, "I did not realize that the verses above said what I just read." The verses called "every spirit" "many false prophets." Verse Three also indicated that "every spirit" (not every mouth) which does not confess that Jesus Christ has come in the flesh … is the spirit of the Antichrist …"

My point, the Antichrist is not the "the beast" as we have been taught. The Antichrist has to do with a "spirit" who works and manifests in and through false prophets (men and women who are beasts in "spirit"). There is a spirit of the

16

Antichrist that energizes the fake prophets in the world. Let me give you a list of the fake prophets in passing. Are you ready!

False prophets are: Firstly, so called men of God whose mouths confess that Jesus Christ came. However, their "spirits" do not confess the same. In other words, there are a lot of preachers who say with their mouths that Jesus came. However, their spirits are dirty with the love of the world (*I John 4:5-6 with I John 2:15-17*). The book of Revelation teaches that the some of the spiritual leaders of the Church would become so dirty there would results in some saints not maturing. The body of Christ is full with a lot of fallen immature followers. They are kept from the Sun Light by fake prophets whose spirits do not confess Jesus.

The other sign that marks the last hour is related to the "plastic" traveling ministers of "another gospel." They are the traveling merchants who are merchandising the saints. They will not travel to Churches unless there is a fee, predetermined or otherwise. Remember, the *"many antichrists"* are marked by traveling—"They went out from us... they went out that they might be made manifest, that none of them were of us" *(1 John 2:19)*. Peter also indicated that false prophets are linked to traveling for the purpose of merchandising the saints.

2 Peter 2:1-3, NKJV: "But there were also false prophets among the people, even as there will be false teachers among you, who ...By covetousness they will exploit (Greek: emporeuomai; English: emporium) you with deceptive (Greek: plastic) words; for a long time, their judgment has not been idle, and their destruction does not slumber."

According to Vines Expository Dictionary, "emporium" literally means to journey in (Gk.; "poros," journey and "en," in); commerce, business, and trade. Strong's Concordance states that emporium means "to travel in as a peddler." The last hour is marked by the traveling of the "many antichrists" who are the "many false prophets." Everyone is claiming to be an apostle or prophet. The last hour is upon us. Babylon's false prophets (merchants) are using the Church for their gain *(compare Revelation 18:10-15).*

Look at the abuse of merchandising the saints, and the abuse of so many traveling about "desiring to be teachers of the law [Word of God], understanding neither what they say nor the things which they affirm" *(1 Timothy 1:7).* The Church has become a marketplace, a sign of the last hour. True men of God are different from the "many." According to Paul, "We are not, as so many, peddling the word of God; but as of sincerity, but as from God, we speak in the sight of God in Christ" *(2 Corinthians 2:17, NKJV).*

Thirdly, false prophets are the psychics of today, palm readers, witches, wizards, those who use charms, necromancy (consulting with the dead), those who use Ouija boards, astrologist, diviners, voodoo, rubbings, drug dealers, etc. Then, some have the nerve to use the name of God in their folly. The apostle Paul called these things ("sorcery") one of the "works of the flesh" *(Galatians 5:20).* God states that people (including some saints) who practice such are the forbidden antagonists of true prophets. They were not to be listened to by true Christians.

Deuteronomy 18:14-15, NKJV: *14For these nations which you will dispossess listened to soothsayers and diviners; but as for you, the LORD your God has not appointed such for you. 15The LORD your God will raise up for you a Prophet [Jesus] like me from your midst, from your brethren. Him you shall hear*

I met a pastor in Baltimore, Maryland who confessed to me that some pastors in the Baltimore area consult diviners to get so called messages for Sunday mornings. (This particular pastor participated in this firsthand.) One pastor, I was told, requested for a voodoo expert to cause the pastor to become the head/presider of a yearly convention in consecutive years. Did you know that according *1 Chronicles 10:13-14* Saul, the first king of Israel, did the same thing, and God killed him for it? Some in the Church are being taught by so called preachers who consult forbidden advisors.

Deuteronomy 18:10-12, NKJV: ¹⁰*There shall not be found among you anyone who makes his son or his daughter pass through the fire, or one, who practices witchcraft, or a soothsayer, or one who interprets omens, or a sorcerer,* ¹¹*or one who conjures spells, or a medium, or a spiritist, or one who calls up the dead.* ¹²*For all who do these things are an abomination to the LORD, and because of these abominations the LORD your God drives them out from before you.*

When God "walks" in His Seven Churches He should not "find" any of the forbidden ones in your assembly, or in your private life. One of the signs of the last hour is the "many false prophets" who indulges in the forbidden secrets of the unclean spirit world. "Beloved, do not believe every spirit … because many false prophets have gone out into the world … this is the spirit of the Antichrist, which you have heard was coming, and is now already in the world" *(1 John 4:1-3, NKJV).*

The land is full of these workers of secret arts, and their presence is the cause for dispossession of property, according to *Deuteronomy, Chapter 18.* Let us judge the illegal spiritists, so that we do not lose our precious land, and be defiled by them. Sorcerers, diviners, and those who use secret crafts defile people and the land. They should be dealt with, according to God's justice. They are antichrists. The book of Ephesians emphatically teaches not to give place to the Devil. Jesus, Paul, and Peter were very swift to deal with those who used secrete arts. They did not have pseudo compassion on the false ones.

Leviticus, 19:31, NKJV: Give no regard to mediums and familiar spirits; do not seek after them, to be defiled by them: I am the LORD your God.

Malachi 3:5, NKJV: And I will come near you for judgment; I will be a swift witness Against sorcerers ... Because they do not fear Me," Says the LORD of hosts.

Acts 13:6-11, NKJV: 6Now when they had gone through the island to Paphos, they found a certain sorcerer, a false prophet, a Jew whose name was Bar-Jesus ... 9Then Saul, who also is called Paul, filled with the Holy Spirit, looked intently at him 10and said, "O full of all deceit and all fraud, you son of the devil, you enemy of all righteousness, will you not cease perverting the straight ways of the Lord? 11And now, indeed, the hand of the Lord is upon you, and you shall be blind, not seeing the sun for a time." And immediately a dark mist fell on him, and he went around seeking someone to lead him by the hand.

The hour hand of man's clock is the shorthand. An hour hand ("shorthand") of the clock of heaven is the Antichrist spirit and the many antichrists that are energized by this spirit. This brings me to my next point! The word for *"last,"* in the phrase, "Little children, it is the last hour" is in nominative case modifying hour. Nominative case names a noun. It means that the word that is designated as nominative bears the name of the noun, "hour." "Last" is an adjective, modifying "hour," a predicate nominative.

In addition, the Greek word for last ("eschatos") is an inflection of "eschatee" and thus acts like a noun. Words in the Greek language that end in suffixes like "tes," "tos," or "tas" attached at the end of them are nouns or acts like nouns. Another way of saying this is the use of a noun (persons, places, or things) usually indicates the idea that is being conveyed.

For example, "teleiotes" for "perfection" in *Hebrews 6:1,* means Perfect One or Finisher; "Christos" for Christ in *Colossians 1:27,* means Anointed One. In *Romans 2:3,* a participle used as a substantive replacing a noun ("prassontas" – "those practicing") from the verb "prasso," or in *Hebrews 10:2* "latreúontas" ("worshipers") is used. In *Hebrews, Chapter 6* where it states, "let us go on to perfection" can read "let us go on to the Perfect One [Jesus]."

Thus, "eschatos" could read the "last one" or "last thing" as a substantive. One of the "last one" that marks the "last hour" is the "Antichrist." (A note in passing for the scholars, I am aware that Jesus is also called the "Eschatos" in *Revelation 22:13,* which is a different topic altogether.)

However, in continuing, another way of saying this is: antichrist (s) is equivalent of the last hour or vice versa. In other words, the Antichrist is an indicator that the hour-hand of the clock is on the "last hour." The spirit of the Antichrist is the last false one to come as the sign of the last hour of this age, and the sign of the last hour of John's age.

This truth, as prophesied by Jesus, was demonstrated in the last years of the last hour of John's time, during the war between the Romans and the Jews (approximately A.D. 66 to A.D. 70). There were false prophets (antichrists according to *1 John 4:1-3*) prophesying rebellion and prophesying false signs, saying that Jerusalem would be delivered from the Romans.

They were prophesying contradictions to Christ's predictions in *Luke 21:20-28.* They were prophesying against what the Christ already said would happen. Thus, Jesus' warning about "false christs" and "false prophets" manifesting themselves before the destruction of Jerusalem was a reality *(Matthew 24:24).*

Antichrists of today also provide false signs to the deceived, saying that the Church will be delivered from an encounter with tribulation and the Beast. The problem with most of these antichrists is they put everything in the future; not realizing a beast exists in every age. What about finding out the ambient time?

When there is a prevalence of antichrists (people or things instead of the true Christ in Churches); (leaders merchandising[6] the people of God); antichrists (people who go to Church, yet in their hearts have forsaken Christ, living a double life), antichrists (those who have revolted against God); and Antichrist (the spirit that energizes the "Jannes and Jambres" types, the "many false prophets," and the "many antichrists") know that the last hour is at hand.

Therefore, the measure of the last hour is not so much duration of time as we know it, as it is the action or personification of those who will leave or speak against the true Graceful One. When a person personifies something that person becomes that thing.

That is, his/her very being screams "antichrist, antichrist, and antichrist." They have the form of Church; yet they personify the corruptible image of worldly man instead of God. There are events happening *"even now"* to show this truth. "Little children, it is the last hour... even now many antichrists have come, by which we know that it is the last hour" *(I John 2:18).*

1 John 2:22, NKJV: Who is a liar but he who denies that Jesus is the Christ? He is antichrist who denies (or lit.; contradicts) the Father and the Son.

Though there are many contradictions against words of the Christ, there are good thing happening in the realm of God.

---

[6] This is not referring to the expected giving as outlined in the Scriptures

Grace always abounds over sin. As one camp sin, God's grace abounds more towards His people. In the overlap of the ages there is a realization taking place in Jesus' disciples concerning God's indestructible life that was already accomplished by Jesus on behalf of the Believers. Therefore, rest in the life of Jesus!

The Overlap

Exodus 36:8-9, NKJV: *⁸Then all the gifted artisans among them who worked on the tabernacle made ten curtains woven of fine linen, and of blue, purple, and scarlet thread; with artistic designs of cherubim, they made them. ⁹The length of each curtain was twenty-eight cubits, and the width of each curtain four cubits; the curtains were all the same size.*

Exodus 36:14-15, NKJV: *¹⁴He made curtains of goats' hair for the tent over the tabernacle; he made eleven curtains. ¹⁵The length of each curtain was thirty cubits, and the width of each curtain four cubits; the eleven curtains were the same size.*

Jesus is seen in all the design of the Tabernacle that Moses built. The reference above typifies Jesus who covers us with "linen" (righteousness). The "blue" can show Jesus as "the heavenly gift." The covering of "goats' hair" shows Jesus as the scapegoat who covers us, and sometimes we are also tagged as goats).

The "purple" shows Jesus as King of kings, and His Church as a royal priesthood. The scarlet thread shows that the blood of Jesus is woven like a thread through our hearts and conscience; and the "designs of cherubim" is too much to speak in detail in this book.

In addition, the curtains also reveal events of God's time. In chapter one of this book, discussion was made concerning the dimensions of the tabernacle that Moses built for the Lord. We saw how the Holy Place (Church Age) was admeasured to be approximately 2,000 years. The Most Holy (the millennium) was admeasured to be approximately 1,000 years.

In like manner, the curtains of the tabernacle sited at the beginning of this chapter, will be used to show that there is a transition between the two ages. I call it the overlap. Note: I do not know the exact date when this overlap started; nor when it will end. However, we can learn the times and seasons from the "pattern" of the tabernacle.

When we look at the tabernacle through the revelation of the Spirit, there is always more that can be understood from the tabernacle. In the Scripture cited at the beginning of this chapter *(Exodus 36:9)*, there were ten curtains, at four cubits wide which covered the tabernacle. When they were grouped together, they total forty (40) cubits.

However, these particular curtains were only 28 cubits long instead of the 30 cubits needed to cover the entire walls of the Tabernacle. This (28 cubits) is incredibly significant. Looking at the front of the tabernacle, the length of the Holy Place, with the height of both sides of the Holy Place were 30 cubits long (10+10+10=30). Thus, the measurement of 28 cubits (9+10+9=28) indicates that this curtain rest approximately one (1) cubit from the bottom of the tabernacle (30-28=2, then divide "2" cubits into equal parts for both sided). The two equal parts are one (1) cubit each [see sketch below].

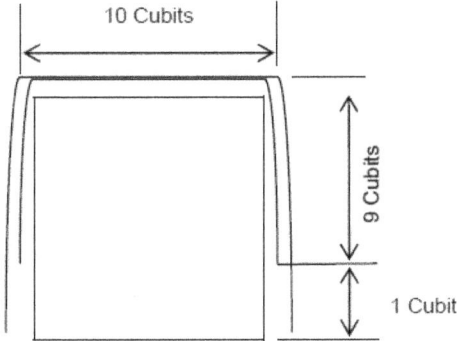

The same is true for the entire tabernacle (the Holy Place and the Most Holy). The entire length, plus the height of the back of the tabernacle, equals forty cubits (30 + 10=40). However, because this particular curtain is held one cubit off the floor at the sides, to keep the curtain uniform, the back also will be held above the ground by one (1) cubit which means that the front had an overhang of one (1) cubit (see sketch below).

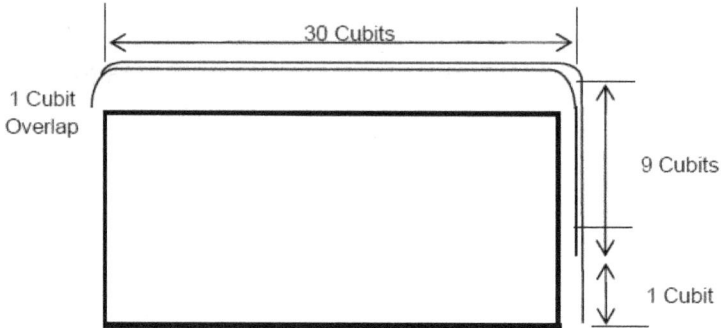

With the previous statements in mind, let us give the significance of the 40 x 28 in relation to time. In the first chapter, we learned that the ages of God relative to His people can be numbered by the tabernacle. The current Church age is reckoned by 10 x 10 x 20=2,000 cubits (years).

Now with the width of the curtain being 28 cubits, the dimensions ("time") is now calculated to be 10 cubits wide x 9 cubits high x 20 cubits long=1800[7] cubits (years), this points to a 200 years difference (overlap) between the two curtains. The other curtain, being 44 cubits long (Exodus 36:14-15), have an overlap of 2 cubits at the front of the tabernacle and 2 cubits at the rear of the tabernacle.

"And you shall double over the sixth curtain at the forefront of the tent… the remnant that remains of the curtains of the tent, the half curtain that remains, shall hang over the back of

---

[7] A study of the 1800s will yield significant historical events relative to the Church.

the tabernacle" *(Exodus 26:9; 12)*. Thus, the 40 cubits left over from the 44 cubits would fit over the assembled tabernacle perfectly. The Millennium is demonstrated by 10 x 10 x 10=1,000 cubits (years). However, with this curtain being shorter, the dimensions now calculate to be 9 x 10 x 10=900 cubits (years). This shows a difference of 100 years from the 1,000 years. Either one hundred years before the new millennium starts, or the first one hundred years in the new millennium, there will be a transition between the kingdom of men and the kingdom of God. The 200 years of the last part of the two thousand years from Jesus, plus the 100 years of the first part of the millennium years total 300 years.

The overlap of the ages is marked by 300 years. Now see a truth! Enoch was translated not to see death after he walked with God for 300 years. He did this around the end of the first millennium.

So likewise, at the end of the sixth (6th) millennium overlapping the start of the seventh (7th) millennium (see the "Timeline" next page), there will be a translation realized as Jesus, Paul and John experienced it. Some people will have the ability to migrate between transfiguration and the natural realm. Jesus did this!

Matthew 17:1-4, NKJV: *1Now after six days Jesus took Peter, James, and John his brother, led them up on a high mountain by themselves; 2 and He was transfigured before them. His face shone like the sun, and His clothes became as white as the light. 3And behold, Moses and Elijah appeared to them, talking with Him.*

2 Corinthians 12:2, NKJV: *2I know a man in Christ who fourteen years ago--whether in the body I do not know, or whether out of the body I do not know, God knows--such a one was caught up to the third heaven.*

27

Revelation 22:8-10, NKJV: *⁸Now I, John, saw and heard these things. And when I heard and saw, I fell down to worship before the feet of the angel who showed me these things. ⁹Then he said to me, "See that you do not do that. For I am your fellow servant, and of your brethren the prophets, and of those who keep the words of this book. Worship God."*

As, the Scriptures above indicated, men have and will be able to migrate between two realms.[8] Jesus through His birthright—the right to birth it first—was translated on the earth, "after six days." If you can receive it, "after six days" is symbolic of a time "after" six thousand years in which there will be a translation.

He was not taken like Enoch and Elijah. Jesus' change happened right here on the earth. Moses and Elijah demonstrated those who were glorified, and yet could manifest themselves in the natural, as God wills.

Paul in like manner did not know if he was in the body (natural realm) or out of the body (spiritual realm) when he met a man who had been to Paradise. The same happened to John in the book of Revelation. The apparent angel that John spoke with was a prophet.

There will be some like Enoch. They will be completely translated as part of their birthright as a witness of the resurrection power of Jesus. I believe this will happen towards the "end" of the three hundred years overlap, whenever God determines that "end" to be.

---

[8] A restoration of what was protected from Adam.

	Enoch's Translation			Jesus' Translation				Birthright Translation
0	1000	2000	3000	4000	5000	6000	7000

Timeline

Genesis 5:22; 24, NKJV: [22]After he begot Methuselah, Enoch walked with God three hundred years... [24]And Enoch walked with God; and he was not, for God took him.

Hebrews 11:5, NKJV: By faith Enoch was taken away so that he did not see death, "and was not found, because God had taken him"; for before he was taken he had this testimony, that he pleased God.

The point is this: the 300 years overlap points to a fulfillment period in which there has begun an experiential change (translation) from one kingdom to another, and it will not happen the way most people think it will. (God will also transfer the kingdom of men to His Son and His Church experientially.)

Enoch was completely delivered from death to ever be with our Lord. Benjamin (son of power, son of the right hand was given 300 pieces of silver (redemption money) by his older brother Joseph (type of Jesus). There will be some "Benjamins" who will be completely redeemed from the power of death. God will take them unto Himself.

Genesis 45:22, NKJV: He gave to all of them, to each man, changes of garments; but to Benjamin he gave three hundred pieces of silver and five changes of garments.

Numbers 3:47-51, NKJV: [47]you shall take five shekels for each one individually; you shall take them in the currency of the shekel of the sanctuary, the shekel of twenty gerahs. [48]And you shall give the money (lit.; silver), with which the excess number of them is redeemed, to Aaron and his sons." [49]So Moses took the redemption

29

money from those who were over and above those who were redeemed by the Levites. ⁵⁰ From the firstborn of the children of Israel he took the money (lit.; silver), one thousand three hundred and sixty-five shekels, according to the shekel of the sanctuary. ⁵¹And Moses gave their redemption money to Aaron and his sons, according to the word of the LORD, as the LORD commanded Moses.

Romans 8:23, NKJV: Not only that, but we also who have the firstfruits of the Spirit, even we ourselves groan within ourselves, eagerly waiting for the adoption, the redemption of our body.

There is a complete (300) redemption (silver) of our bodies that will be accomplished by Jesus. It is called translation into an age that already exists. He foreran "into the age" waiting for us to do the same. Those who are victorious will sit with Jesus in/on the right hand of His throne.

Revelation 3:21, NKJV: To him who overcomes I will grant to sit with Me on My throne, as I also overcame and sat down with My Father on His throne.

One of the measures of a mature Believer is to strive for the resurrection from among the living dead. Yet, there are some people who are more interested in the dead rather than the living Church. Every Sunday, they have someone to bury. There must be a resurrection from among the dead.

Matthew 8:22, NKJV: But Jesus said to him, "Follow Me, and let the dead bury their own dead."

Philippians 3:10-11, NKJV: ¹⁰that I may know Him and the power of His resurrection, and the fellowship of His sufferings, being conformed to His death, ¹¹ if, by any means, I may attain to the resurrection from (Gk.; "ek", out of) the dead.

Philippians 3:14-15: NKJV: ¹⁴I press toward the goal for the prize of the upward call of God in Christ Jesus. ¹⁵Therefore let us, as many as are mature, have this mind; and if in anything you think otherwise, God will reveal even this to you.

Some must enter in the promised "today" *(Hebrews 4)*. Jesus stated that there is a difference between those who die and are raised again from the dead, and those who never die (good study). We are in the overlap, and some will not sleep in death – "… We shall not all sleep, but we shall be changed" *(1 Corinthians 15:51)*.

For those who believe that a translation without death is not possible. Listen to the Holy Writ: "Elijah was a man with a nature like ours …" *(James 5:17)*; and "… Elijah went up by a whirlwind into heaven" *(2 Kings 2:11)*. A problem with some is that maybe some people think that they have to do the work. Therefore, they disbelieve; because they feel their nature disqualifies them. Not true! Elijah had a "nature" like ours, yet the Lord took him up. The translation is always performed by God not man. Adam was translated to Eden by the "Lord God." Enoch was taken by "God," Elijah was taken into heaven by "Lord."

2 Kings 2:1, NKJV: And it came to pass, when the LORD was about to take up Elijah into heaven by a whirlwind, that Elijah went with Elisha from Gilgal.

Genesis 5:24, NKJV: And Enoch walked with God; and he was not, for God took him.

Do you see it? All you have to do is believe. It will be Jesus "Who will transform our lowly body that it may be conformed to His glorious body …" *(Philippians 3:21)*. Caleb was kept alive by "the Lord" for forty-five years before Caleb inherited his promised land, and he testified how he was "as strong this day as on the day Moses sent me" *(Joshua 14:10-11)*.

Caleb was eighty-five years old when he began the process of possessing his land of promise. Our Lord Jesus is full of endless life. At any time, He chooses He can cause us to live extended or translated lives right here on earth. He can change our mortal bodies to be just like His — energized by the life-giving spirit.

In conclusion, this overlap will be glorious, yet intense for the Saints. According to Paul, in *Philippians 3:10:* sufferings are linked with the Saints ability to partake of Jesus' resurrection power. There will be intensified suffering during the season of translation from one age "into the age" of the indestructible life according to the order of Melchizedek.

I believe this will happen during the season of the overlap of the ages, as two families (light and darkness) mature simultaneously. The sanctuary will then be made "right" (Hebrew: "tsedeq" — zedek) by Melchizedek (Jesus) and His order. Melchizedek being translated from the Hebrew language as the "King of Right or Righteousness" (Hebrew: "tsedeq"). The Wonderful One has declared this.

Wonderful One

*Daniel 8:13-14, NKJV: [13]Then I heard a **holy one** speaking; and another **holy one** said to that certain one who was speaking, "How long will the vision be, concerning the daily sacrifices and the transgression of desolation, the giving of both the sanctuary and the host to be trampled underfoot?" [14]And he said to me, "For two thousand three hundred days; then the sanctuary shall be cleansed."*

Jesus is that "certain one" typified in the text above, in addition to that "holy one" being one of the "watchers" over the affairs of kings and their kingdoms *(Daniel 4)*. This holy one or certain one has the answer as to the durations or the measure of God's time. God has a measure for an "hour" under heaven, just like man has developed a method to tract the seconds, minutes, and hours in a day. As shown in the chapter on "the last hour," I demonstrated that God's hours are manifested by events, persons, and duration.

In this chapter, I will continue the development of God's hour from a Person. His name is Jesus. I will then conclude with "persons" who will also personify "two thousand three hundred days (lit.; evening-mornings)."

Daniel saw a vision, and in the vision a "holy one" inquired as to the duration of this particular vision – "How long will the vision be …." The reply came by another spiritual being, named as "that certain one." In addition, "that certain one" gave the duration of "two thousand three hundred days."

The name "that certain one" is from the Hebrew word "Palmowniy." The etymology of the word is from two roots. It is derived from an obsolete noun, paalown, and/or from the verb paalaah, to distinguish, put a difference, show marvelous, separate, set apart, sever, make wonderfully (see Strong's Concordance), and is united with the word "almoniy," which means one concealed , unknown one, silent

33

one or secret one. From these definitions, I will use one combination to develop my point.

First, the Secret One or Wonderful One that Palmowniy can represent is Jesus. The Scriptures always testify of Jesus *(John 5:39)*. Therefore, we must always look for the person of Jesus. Paul preached Jesus.

Isaiah 9:6, NKJV: For unto us a Child is born, Unto us a Son is given; And the government will be upon His shoulder. And His name will be called Wonderful, Counselor, Mighty God, Everlasting Father, Prince of Peace.

Jesus was also the mystery (secret) of God *(Colossians 2:2; Revelation 10:7)* who was revealed in the New Testament. His name is called Wonderful, as we just saw above. In addition, He is also the mystery revealed. Thus, Palmowniy (Wonderful Secret) is found in the uncovering of Jesus Christ.

Revelation 10:7, NKJV: But in the days when the seventh angel is about to sound his trumpet, the mystery of God will be accomplished, just as he announced to his servants the prophets ...

Colossians 2:2, NKJV: That their hearts may be encouraged, being knit together in love, and attaining to all riches ... of the mystery of God, both of the Father and of Christ ....

Colossians 2:2, NIV: My purpose is that they may be encouraged in heart and united in love, so that they may have the full riches of complete understanding, in order that they may know the mystery of God, namely, Christ ...

The mystery of God is Christ. Jesus Christ was the Secret Wonderful One that is now revealed. In addition, the translation of the name of Palmowniy is witnessed in the book of *Hebrews, Chapter 7*. The writer of Hebrews used the translation of the name of Melchizedek to bring out truth concerning Jesus. Melchizedek is a composition of two word, Melek (King) and tsedeq (righteousness or right).

Hebrews 7:1-2, NKJV: ¹For this Melchizedek, king of Salem, priest of the Most High God, who met Abraham returning from the slaughter of the kings and blessed him, ² to whom also Abraham gave a tenth part of all, first being translated "king of righteousness," and then also king of Salem, meaning "king of peace."

The same is true for the Hebrew word translated "Palmowniy." One of the "translations" is "Wonderful Secret." Who and what is this "Wonderful Secret?" As stated before, the "Who" is Jesus!

The "what," in context of the definition of Palmowniy, is the wonderful secret that was hidden in the answer to the question asked by the other holy one, "How long ...?" Palmowniy (a type of the Wonderful One — Jesus) responded by saying "two thousand three hundred days."

These "days" that were specified in the answer are also called a "pattern" *(Daniel 8:26)*. This word "pattern" is the same word used by Moses and David with respect to the *"pattern"* they were given by the Lord to build the Tabernacle built by Moses and Temple built by Solomon, respectively.

Thus, there is truth ready to be uncovered in the answer given by Palmowniy. "How long will the vision be ...?" "For two thousand three hundred days...." The Hebrew text can alternately read: "For two thousand (or lit; two families, two oxen) three hundred evening (or lit; Arabia, mixed people) morning (or lit; dawn)."

Therefore, in the numerals of "two thousand three hundred" there is a literal meaning. There is also a "wonderful" meaning from the "pattern" in the "translation" of the words. Remember, Melchizedek's name is "translated" to mean "King of Righteousness" as demonstrated in *Hebrews 7:1-2.*

35

Hebrews 7:1-2, NKJV: *¹For this Melchizedek, king of Salem, priest of the Most High God, who met Abraham returning from the slaughter of the kings and blessed him, ²to whom also Abraham gave a tenth part of all, first being translated "king of righteousness," and then also king of Salem, meaning "king of peace."*

Definition can clarify ignorance. Thus, another way of looking at the duration in which the daily sacrifice will be affected, and the duration of the desolation cause by transgressions are by the meaning of the words used by a representative of the Word Himself—Palmowniy. God speaks by threes, and the "three hundred days" are "words of truth" that are symbolic "patterns."

Proverbs 22:20-21, NKJV: *²⁰Have I not written to you excellent things (lit.; triple or threefold things) Of counsels and knowledge, ²¹ That I may make you know the certainty of the words of truth, That you may answer words of truth To those who send to you?*

There are "threefold" stages of growth: children, young men, and fathers *(1 John 2:12-14)*; threefold Tent of Meeting: Outer Court, Holy Place, and Holiest of All; there is the threefold man: spirit, soul, and body, etc. The Godhead is manifested in three—"⁹ For in Him dwells all the fullness of the Godhead bodily; ¹⁰ and you are complete in Him, who is the head of all principality and power."*(Colossians 2:9-10)*.

Therefore, the "three" in the phrase "three hundred" evening and mornings" points to the fullness, mature or completion of the things stated in the verse of *Daniel 8:14*. In this case, "two families" or "two oxen" must come to a place of "three one hundred". "One hundred," according to Jesus, points to the yielding of "fruit" or the yielding of a "crop"

Mark 4:8, NKJV: *But other seed fell on good ground and yielded a crop (or, fruit) that sprang up, increased, and produced: some thirtyfold, some sixty, and some a hundred …*

There must be a maturity (three) of fruit (one hundred) of "two families" who will look like "two oxen." There is only one difference from the two families or the two oxen. One will be of the morning (dawn), and the other will be of the evening (dusk). Jesus is the "Morning Star" who will dawn through us. The Saints of the Most High were birthed from the womb of the morning.

2 Peter 1:19, NKJV: And so, we have the prophetic word confirmed, which you do well to heed as a light that shines in a dark place, until the day dawns and the morning star rises in your hearts

Revelation 22:16, NKJV: I, Jesus, have sent My angel to testify to you these things in the churches. I am the Root and the Offspring of David, the Bright and Morning Star."

The Believers in Jesus are called sons of the day and sons of the light. "You are all sons of the light and sons of the day ..." *(1 Thessalonians 5:5a)*; and we came from "the womb of the morning" *(Psalm 110:3)*. The Church is the morning who shall mature in "three" seasons to be a "fruitful" bough by the well.

The "evening" is of an interesting sort. First, the Hebrew word translated as "evening" is also translated as "mixed people," "mingled people," "web or traverses of threads of cloth," "mixture" and "Arabia." The mixture is a pattern of all the mixture that will be in some Churches and the world in the last of these days. Babylon means mixed confusion (see Strong's #894 and #1101; *Revelation 17-18*).

There will be a complete maturity ("three") of the fruitfulness (one hundred-fold) of mixed religion in the earth. In addition, at the same time, the children of the day are also maturing. Another way of saying this is, as Jesus indicated: When the wheat matures with its fruit, the tares also appear with the wheat.

Matthew 13:24-26, NKJV: *[24]Another parable He put forth to them, saying: "The kingdom of heaven is like a man who sowed good seed in his field; [25]but while men slept, his enemy came and sowed tares among the wheat and went his way. [26] But when the grain had sprouted and produced a crop, then the tares also appeared.*

Therefore, the maturity of both light and darkness is the scale by which the duration in *Daniel 8:13* can be measured. Do you see this? The antichrists of today have made God's heritage full of mixture; they are the "evenings," and they will be cleansed from the sanctuary through the morning light *(Daniel 8:14).*The "shadows" of the night "flee away" when the "day breaks" *(see Song of Solomon 4:6).* The evening may also point to the Arabic based religions which will be maturing simultaneously against the "pure religion" *(James 1:27)* of God. The word evening ("ereb") is also translated as "Arabia" in *1 Kings 10:15.*

1 Kings 10:15:, NKJV: Besides that from the traveling merchants, from the income of traders, from all the kings of Arabia (lit; haa-`Ereb), and from the governors of the country.

I do not say this as if there is no hope for the salvation of those of the Arabic based religions. I am also not saying all Arabs are against Christians. In fact, the power of the gospel will also save the Arabic nations. The true Light will also dawn on them. Salvation is for every nation (see below), and every kingdom will become our Lord's and His Christ. However, everyone knows that Islam was founded in Arabia approximately six hundred years after Jesus.

Acts 2:7-11, NKJV: [7]Then they were all amazed and marveled, saying to one another, "Look, are not all these who speak Galileans? [8]And how is it that we hear, each in our own language in which we were born? [9] Parthians and Medes and Elamites, those dwelling in Mesopotamia, Judea and Cappadocia, Pontus and Asia, [10]Phrygia and Pamphylia, Egypt and the parts of Libya adjoining Cyrene, visitors from Rome, both Jews and proselytes, [11]Cretans and Arabs — we hear them speaking in our own tongues the wonderful works of God."

Acts 2:37, NKJV: Now when they heard this, they were cut to the heart, and said to Peter and the rest of the apostles, "Men and brethren, what shall we do?"

Habakkuk 2:14, NKJV: For the earth will be filled with the knowledge of the glory of the LORD, as the waters cover the sea

The hope is that some may read this book and ask, "what shall we do" to be saved. I speak the truth that the Church may not be swayed. Islam was birthed in Arabia. Thus, any nation, black or white, that embraces Islam, their belief is now "ereb" based.

I was told a few years ago that many of the Nation of Islam in America are former Christians, especially Baptist. Hence, this duality constitutes mixture. I believe the "evening" points to the evening hour of this age when conflicts will be prevalent between all the religions of "mixture" against the Christians. There will be a lot of religion "mixing" with each other which will result in persecution of the "pure religion."

Finally, I will briefly discuss the interpretation of the "two oxen" of the "evening" and the "morning." The ox points to the sweet-smelling sacrifice of God *(Leviticus 1)*. Jesus is our Ox of sweet-smelling sacrifice for us towards God *(Ephesians 5:2)*. He was slaughtered instead of us and for us.

Similarly, in the context of *Daniel 8:13-14,* the two oxen point to the fact that in the latter days, the sons of the darkness (all religions except for the Church of Jesus) and the sons of the morning (mature Believers) will both be claiming martyrdom (being slaughtered like an ox). This truth is also described in the book of Revelation. However, there is only One who can claim to be an Ox—Jesus and His Church. Yet, Babylon will be martyred by the beast?

Revelation 17:16, NKJV: And the ten horns which you saw on (Gk; kai — and also) the beast, these will hate the harlot [Babylon], make her desolate and naked, eat her flesh and burn her with fire.

There are many religions that claim martyrdom when they are persecuted by the beast system. An odd thing is that false religions get attention when they claim to be killed for their belief. However, when the true Church gets martyred, it is sometimes difficult for some to acknowledge that some modern Christians are indeed being slaughtered for a noble cause.

The overlap of the ages will also be marked by all religions claiming martyrdom. Therefore, do not be confused when other religions claim they are being martyred for their beliefs. It is part of the bait of Satan to minimize the "pure religion" of the Church

The duration of the two thousand three hundred days are marked by the fact of conflicts between two opposite families in the earth as they reach maturity in their respective beliefs. The Church must not waver from Jesus, the Day Star. He will eventually dawn through our hearts to counter the darkness that is manifesting itself through those who choose the mixed way.

There are so called Churches in the mixed way. Everything is allowed in order to keep membership and acquire money. However, there is a limit for everything. The sanctuary shall be "made right" after "two thousand evenings and mornings." Yet, God's determination of when the end finally comes seems to always override man's timetable.

It follows that the "two thousand three hundred evening-mornings" also typify a "pattern" of events to be fulfilled in the last days. Peter said the prophets thought they prophesied about "themselves" when in reality they prophesied about Christ's sufferings and the glories (us) that were to follow Him. "Of this salvation the prophets have inquired ... and searching ... what manner of time ... the sufferings of Christ and the glories that would follow. To them it was revealed that, not unto themselves, but to us they were ministering ..." (1 Peter 1:10-12).

Another way of saying this is: God sometimes extends events, as only He knows why. The Lord did this in Daniel's book with respect to Jeremiah's prophecy of the seventy years captivity. Jeremiah and Daniel thought that the prophecy of seventy years of desolation was just that, seventy years. However, the prophecy of the desolation of Jerusalem was also meant for another period. The apparent seventy years were expanded to be four hundred and ninety years.

Seventy Times Seven

Daniel 9:2, NKJV: In the first year of his reign I, Daniel, understood by the books the number of the years specified by the word of the LORD through Jeremiah the prophet, that He would accomplish seventy years in the desolations of Jerusalem.

Jesus is the key to understanding any of the books of the Bible. The preceding chapter opened to us the role of the Wonderful One who gives understanding of "patterns" as they relate to times and seasons. God knows all things.

In this chapter, we will see how our Messiah is also linked to understanding "by the books" the expansion of the seventy years to four hundred and ninety years. Jesus is the Word, and no one knows the word like Him.

Revelation 19:12-13, NKJV: [12]His eyes were like a flame of fire, and on His head were many crowns. He had a name written that no one knew except Himself. [13]He was clothed with a robe dipped in blood, and His name is called The Word of God.

Jesus had a name that no one really knows except Himself. His name is the Word of God. Jesus knows His name (Word) inside out. Any questions you have, the Word will answer, except, the date when He is coming physically. The book of Hebrews said everything about Jesus is written in the volume of the Book.

Hebrews 10:5-7, NKJV: [5]Therefore, when He came into the world, He said: "Sacrifice and offering You did not desire, But a body You have prepared for Me. [6]In burnt offerings and sacrifices for sin You had no pleasure. [7]Then I said, 'Behold, I have come — In the volume of the book it is written of Me — To do Your will, O God.'"

As, indicated earlier, the Greek word for "of" is "peri," and it means all about, all around. It is used in the English words perimeter and periscope. The perimeter of an object is the measure all around the edges.

In the Bible, everything about Jesus is in the book. Daniel understood this. He indicated that he "understood by the books the number of the years specified by the word of the LORD through Jeremiah the prophet, that He would accomplish seventy years in the desolations of Jerusalem."

It is possible to understand durations relative to the Israel of God (the Church). The Bible is the answer. Daniel understood time by the book of Jeremiah. It is from this point of view — the explanation to Daniel what the seventy years actually meant — I will develop a perspective of God's hour under heaven (in eternity time is infinite) in the subsequent chapter.

Daniel 9:20-23, NKJV: [20]*Now while I was speaking, praying, and confessing my sin and the sin of my people Israel, and presenting my supplication before the LORD my God for the holy mountain of my God,* [21] *yes, while I was speaking in prayer, the man Gabriel, whom I had seen in the vision at the beginning, being caused to fly swiftly, reached me about the time of the evening offering.* [22] *And he informed me, and talked with me, and said, "O Daniel, I have now come forth to give you skill to understand.* [23] *At the beginning of your supplications the command went out, and I have come to tell you, for you are greatly beloved; therefore, consider the matter, and understand the vision:*

Daniel began to pray after he read Jeremiah's notes concerning the seventy years desolation. During the prayer, Gabriel was sent by God to give Daniel understanding. The seventy years is about to expanded to four hundred and ninety years.

This concept is vital to understand the "hour of God." In the New Testament there will also be what I call an expansion of time. This may be applied to the ratio of God's hour relative to His Day. This expansion of time is also applicable to the forty-two months of the beast's system rule.

Daniel 9:24, NKJV: Seventy weeks (lit; seven) are determined for your people and for your holy city, to finish the transgression, to make an end of sins, to make reconciliation for iniquity, to bring in everlasting righteousness, to seal up vision and prophecy, and to anoint the Most Holy.

"Seventy weeks" are Jeremiah's seventy years prophecy multiplied by seven (70 x 7=490 years). I wonder what went through Daniel's mind. Seventy years is a long time, and the angel Gabriel expanded the seventy years into three phases to reach four hundred and ninety years.

Daniel 9:25, NKJV: Know therefore and understand, That from the going forth of the command To restore and build Jerusalem Until Messiah the Prince, There shall be seven weeks and sixty-two weeks; The street shall be built again, and the wall, Even in troublesome times.

In this verse, we see two of the phases. There is seven weeks (7 x 7=49 years). There are also sixty-two weeks (62 x 7=434 years). He then follows in the next verse by saying that after the sixty-two weeks, the Messiah will be covenanted.

Daniel 9:26, NKJV: And after the sixty-two weeks Messiah shall be cut off (or lit; covenanted, Haggai 2:5), but not for Himself; And the people of the prince who is to come Shall destroy the city and the sanctuary. The end of it shall be with a flood, And till the end of the war desolations are determined.

"After" the sixty-two sevens (the forty-nine years plus the four hundred and thirty-four years), Jesus was "covenanted" for the New Covenant. The word "cut off" means to covenant by means of cutting flesh in two pieces where blood flows and then pass between the cut fleshes.

Jesus was cut for us. His blood is the blood of the New Covenant. Jesus was sacrificed for us "after" the sixty-two sevens. This period is the final seven of the seventy sevens (490 years).

Daniel 9:27, NKJV: Then he shall confirm (Heb.; strengthen) a covenant with many for one week; But in the middle of the week, He shall bring an end to sacrifice and offering. And on the wing of abominations shall be one who makes desolate, Even until the consummation, which is determined, Is poured out on the desolate.

Jesus "confirmed (lit; strengthened)" the New Covenant in the final week; and he ended animal sacrifice by His sacrifice in the middle of this final week. This seventieth week is the third period of the four hundred and ninety years [(49 years (1st period), 434 years (2nd period) and 7 years (the 3rd period)].

In all that was said above, I wanted to demonstrate that God's reserves the right to reveal His expanded plan when He feels ready. The seventy years became seventy times seven, or four hundred and ninety years. God also demonstrates this principle of expansion of durations by the year day principle.

When Israel spied out the promise land for forty days, most did not return with a good report. God judged them and stated that they shall bear their iniquity for forty years, a year for a day. In this case, man is a variable of time. God's intention was for a quick rout to the promise land. However, man's unbelief extended the duration. Thus, as stated before, man is a variable of time.

Numbers 14:33-34, NKJV: 33And your sons shall be shepherds in the wilderness forty years, and bear the brunt of your infidelity, until your carcasses are consumed in the wilderness. 34 According to the number of the days in which you spied out the land, forty days, for each day you shall bear your guilt one year, namely forty years, and you shall know My rejection.

The words of this Scripture are strong. A year for a day was the verdict for unbelief. God has a habit of expanding time. In this case, the reason was man's "infidelity." Yet, the principle stands sure; time can be expanded or contracted to mean more than we originally think it means.

Ezekiel also carried the iniquity of the people for days which were expanded to point to the years that the people themselves would bear their own iniquity. Three hundred and ninety days really meant three hundred and ninety years. Forty days were expanded to be forty years when fulfilled in the people's lives.

Ezekiel 4:4-6; NKJV: ⁴*"Lie also on your left side and lay the iniquity of the house of Israel upon it. According to the number of the days that you lie on it, you shall bear their iniquity.* ⁵*For I have laid on you the years of their iniquity, according to the number of the days, three hundred and ninety days; so, you shall bear the iniquity of the house of Israel.* ⁶*And when you have completed them, lie again on your right side; then you shall bear the iniquity of the house of Judah forty days. I have laid on you a day for each year.*

My purpose for this chapter was not to discuss in detail the aspects of the four hundred and ninety years, but to show that the seventy years prophesied by Jeremiah were expanded by God to four hundred and ninety years. It was to demonstrate by example that days can be expanded to be years. Understand the mystery.

God will reveal certain durations to his apostles and prophets. He will then wait until the fulfillment of the duration draws near to give His expanded (explained version) of His plan. The expanded version has always been His plan. God likes to keep certain secrets until He is ready to reveal them.

Matthew 17:9, NKJV: Now as they came down from the mountain, Jesus commanded them, saying, "Tell the vision[9] to no one until the Son of Man is risen from the dead."

Revelation 10:4, NKJV: Now when the seven thunders uttered their voices, I was about to write; but I heard a voice from heaven saying to me, "Seal up the things which the seven thunders uttered, and do not write them."

The same is true for other things in the New Testament. That which was once designated to remain hidden is now being revealed. Let us look at what I call the first hour of the overlap towards the new millennium. I am not convinced that the new millennium has started. We are still in the overlap. I remember the great panic before the year two thousand (Y2K). Our Church was full that New Year's Eve.

I indicated to the Church and fearful guests that nothing would happen, and that we had at least another thirty-three years, minimum, before the new millennium starts. The year two-thousand passed; and we are still here.

Nothing changed in the natural as yet, so people are mocking the lies some in the Church has propagated *(2 Peter 3:2-4)*. Yes, the millennium age will be realized; however, I believe the first hour and/or the first one hundred years towards the millennium will be a significant period.

---

[9] Please refer to my book *Vision Real* for further development

The First Hour

Revelation 17:12, NKJV: The ten horns which you saw are ten kings who have received no kingdom as yet, but they receive authority for one hour as kings with the beast.

Jesus is the one who ordains things in the earth. Nothing happens without His knowing. "God has put it into their hearts to fulfill His purpose, to be of one mind, and to give their kingdom to the beast, until the words of God are fulfilled" *(Revelation 17:17)*. Yet, in the mind of some in the western world are concerns about the rapture of the Church, the mark of the Beast, and the Beast himself (itself).

There is an hour of this Beast and its ten horns. But the Lord is fully aware of its existence and effect. This beast and its ten friends are only allowed one hour, and to be more specific they have only the first hour; "they receive authority for one (lit; first) hour as kings with the beast."

When is this first hour? The first hour always comes after the last hour. If the last hour is 12:00 PM, then the first hour after 12:00 PM is 1:00 AM. The first hour is after the last hour. As indicated above, the Greek word for "one" ("mian") also means "first" as an ordinal as can be seen in the references below.

Matthew 28:1, NKJV: Now after the Sabbath, as the first (Gk; mian) day of the week began to dawn, Mary Magdalene and the other Mary came to see the tomb.

Titus 3:10, NKJV: Reject a divisive man after the first (Gk; mian) and second admonition…

Thus, the resurrected head of the beast (the eighth beast "out of" seven that existed before) with its ten horns rules in the first hour of an era after the last hour, to "fulfill His [God's] purpose." The beast system exists in every age.

However, in the first hour before the new millennium (whenever that is), or in the beginning of the new millennium (again, whenever that is), the eighth beast will be personified or created again out of one of the previous seven heads.

We are currently in the overlap of the ages. And again, for emphasis, I do not claim to know the exact day when the overlap starts or ends. That would be foolish to predict.

In fact, when one studies the timing of God's events, most of the time one is still left with the question, "when O Lord?" However, the "times" and "seasons" are revealed by the Word and the Holy [Clean] Spirit.

In the chapter, "The Last Hour," discussion was made as to the personification of the last hour. The last hour is revealed by the "Antichrist" and the "many antichrists." The Antichrist, as we learned, is really the "spirit" behind the many false prophets, and this spirit is called "the false Prophet."

The same is also true for the Beast. The first hour is marked by a personification of the beast system. The beast existed since the days of Babylon until now (Daniel 7, etc.). In every age, there was a beast and its system that ruled society. When John saw the vision of the beast, he indicated that "one" of the heads (kings) of the beast lived in his day.

Revelation 17:7, NKJV: 7But the angel said to me, "Why did you marvel? I will tell you the mystery of the woman and of the beast that carries her, which has the seven heads and the ten horns.

Revelation 17:9-10, NKJV: 9Here is the mind which has wisdom: The seven heads are seven mountains on which the woman sits. 10 There are also seven kings. Five have fallen, one is, and the other has not yet come. And when he comes, he must continue a short time.

Note: the beast lived in the days of John—"one is," and John was not influenced by the mark of the beast, or the image of the beast, neither the beast's name nor number. John showed that it is possible to live in the age of a beast system and not take the mark of the beast.

Stop being afraid! The Prophet Daniel was not marked by the beasts of Babylon, or the beast of the Medes or the Persians (Daniel 1:8 w/Daniel 2:38; Daniel 7:4). There is a "victory" over any beasts and their systems.

A beast system also lives now. No one has to either take or receive its mark *(Revelation 15:1-4)*. However, I also understand that the beast will be personified in the first hour through those who are deceived by the beastly nature in mankind *(Ecclesiastes 3:18)*.

For example, the beast is being personified by people changing their very bodies to fit what I call "the image expectancy" of this beastly age. This image expectancy is both mental and physical. The personification of the beast includes, but is not limited to, humanity becoming the image of the invisible beast *(Revelation 13:14)*, as Christ is the image of the invisible God *(Colossians 1:15)*.

Revelation 13:11-15, NKJV: *[11]Then I saw another beast coming up out of the earth ... [12]And he exercises all the authority of the first beast in his presence ... [13]He performs great signs ... [14]And he deceives those who dwell on the earth by those signs which he was granted to do in the sight of the beast, telling those who dwell on the earth to make **an image** to the beast who was wounded by the sword and lived. [15]He was granted power to give **breath (lit.; spirit)** to the image of the beast, that the image of the beast should both speak and cause as many as would not worship the image of the beast to be killed.*

The beast system of this age is causing people to cut their bodies to fit the "image expectancy" of this age. This "image expectancy" has a voice; because "the image of the beast … speaks and killed." The voice of the beast's image comes into the minds via "spirit" and the death of peer pressure (relational death threats for not following the "norm"). The voice says, "Cut your body to make it an image that fits the expectancy of others (including the invisible (spirit) image beast).

The norm is: plastic surgery to have the right image. What is the saying? "Image is everything!" Yes and they are making themselves god *(2 Thessalonians 2:4; 1 Corinthians 6:13, last part)*. God made a rule against people changing their body image. In the same breath, he stated *"I am the Lord."*

No one has the lordship to change their image, except God; and the only image that the Lord will change is a person distorted image of him/her selves. Did you know the Bible teaches that the Lord made you "fearfully" so as to make you exactly as you are? Therefore, when people change their "born" image, they are acting like God.

Leviticus 19:28, NKJV: You shall not make any cuttings in your flesh for the dead (lit.; soul), nor tattoo any marks (lit.; marked or branded incision) on you: I am the LORD.

The "soul" of humanity is not content with God's image. They prefer to make an image "to" the beast. Note: *Revelation 13:14* did not say they made an image "for" the beast, but an image "to" the beast. There is a difference. They are actually personifying the beast.

However, in continuing on with the topic, I will develop the duration of an hour and then apply that to the first hour relative to the beast. We learned in the previous chapter that time can be reckoned by events, people, expanded durations, etc. The same is true for the duration of one hour. It may be expanded.

2 Peter 3:8, NKJV: But, beloved, do not forget this one thing, that with the Lord one day is as a thousand years, and a thousand years as one day.

Many people called Peter unlearned. Yet he was the one that God gave the understanding of God's day. Why was this possible? He spent time "with Jesus" *(Acts 4:13)*. My point is Jesus teaches us today. The Word of God is alive and active today *(Hebrews 4:12)*. He is "with" us today.

Why is spending time "with" the Lord so important? Peter stated that one day "with" (Greek "para" defined as "near") the Lord is "as a thousand years." When we stay "near" the Lord, we walk in the power of the "millennium" age, now. This is one of the secrets of the millennium (Holy of Holies) rule.

Yet, there is more. "One day is as one thousand years." There are twenty-four (24) hours in one full day. Thus, there are also twenty-four hours in the one thousand years (a day of God). Do you see this? It is important that this concept is understood because we have to do some simple math.

To get the duration that equates to one hour for one thousand years, we have to divide the thousand years (one day) by twenty-four hours (1000/24=41.67 years) which equals 41.67 years. This is rounded to 42 years.

The beast reigned for one (1) hour; that is, 42 years; or another way of saying this is: there is a forty-second generation of the beast's reign (see Chapter 7 of this book for details on the forty-first and forty second generations of Christ).

That is, the beast system that exists in the era of the Church will only last for approximately forty-two generations (~2,000

52

years). The beast existed in the days when John saw the visions of the book of Revelation, and it still exists. Some might ask, "What about the 42 months (3 ½ years) of the beast's reign?" That will be discussed next.

This duration of approximately forty-two years and/or forty-two generations, in lieu of the forty-two months, should not be strange. Remember, Daniel thought that the seventy years desolation prophesied by Jeremiah was just that, seventy years. However, God, through Gabriel (apostolic angel), showed that the seventy years are indeed four hundred and ninety years. The same is true for the forty-two months the beast will reign. The forty-two months can be "translated" to depict forty-two years, and/or forty-two generations.

Earlier, we saw that 1000/24=41.67 years, rounded to 42 years. This "42 years" also points to forty-two generations over a span of approximately 2,000 years. (The forty-two generations from Abraham to Christ were approximately 2,000 years.) The second witness is as follows.

Revelation 13:5, NKJV: And he was given a mouth speaking great things and blasphemies, and he was given authority to continue for forty-two months.

Forty-two months are equal to three and a half years. In *Daniel, Chapter 9,* the governing number used for expansion is "seven." In the New Testament relative to the Church, the number twelve plays an important role. The original government of the Church was administered by the twelve apostles. At the same time, I am not minimizing the importance of seven or any other numbers[10] in the Word of God.

---

[10] A word of caution: please do not to go overboard with numbers.

There are twelve apostles of the Lamb *(Revelation 21:14)*. The measure of the wall of the City is one hundred and forty-four, which is twelve squared — 12^2 *(Revelation 21:17)*. The total measure of New Jerusalem is twelve thousand furlongs — Gk.; stadia, Eng.; stadium *(Revelation 21:16)*.

There are twelve gates for the City, New Jerusalem *(Revelation 21: 12)*. Those who follow the Lamb on Mount Zion are one hundred forty-four thousand, which is twelve thousand multiplied by twelve — 12000 x 12 =144,000 *(Revelation 14:1)*. There are twelve stars on the head of the woman *(Revelation 12:1)*.

Finally, in *John 11:9-10,* Jesus distinguished the day from the night by saying there are twelve hours for the daylight. Thus, by interpolation, there are also twelve hours for the night — "the evening and the morning were the first day" *(Genesis 1:5)*.

"Jesus answered, "Are there not twelve hours in the day? ... But if one walks in the night, he stumbles ..." *(John 11:9-10)*. The "hours" of the daylight are characterized by the number "twelve." Jesus is the Light; and we are in His daylight.

Jesus is the Governor (as depicted by the number twelve) of all the heavens, the sea, and the earth and under the earth. To reiterate, Jeremiah's seventy years were increased by a multiple of seven. There is an extension of the 42 months, or 3 ½ years by a multiple of twelve (the Day Light of Jesus), and the numbers will match.

One thousand divided by twenty-four hours in a full day is approximately forty-two (1000/24=41.67 or ~42). It follows that three and a half years (3 ½) multiplied by twelve (12) also equals forty-two years (3.5 years x 12=42 years). This value matches God's hours relative to the one-thousand-year day principle. Do you see it? God declared the entire reign of the beast with its ten horns to be one hour *(see Revelation 17: 12)*. One hour of what?

One hour of His one thousand year-day principle *(2 Peter 3)*. This is a relatively short time in a thousand-year period. In other words, one hour of a millennium is approximately forty-two years. This equates to three and a half years being expanded by twelve, similarly to Jeremiah's seventy years being extended by seven to become four hundred and ninety, in *Daniel 9*.

The third witness is that the Greek word for "month" in "forty-two months" is an inflection of "men" ("meénas") which means "measure" according to Vines Expository Dictionary. Thus, the forty-two months may be translated to mean forty-two measures. The measures can range from forty-two months (literally) to forty-two years when "measures" are equated to "twelve."

In addition, the forty-two measures, also point to forty-two generations of the beast's war against the Saints, starting from the generation of Jesus (i.e., approximately 2,000 years ago) until the iron and the clay kingdom crumble completely. How did I get this 2000 years duration? The answer is: According to the Bible, the time from Abraham to Christ was forty-two generations (14 + 14 + 14=42), which was approximately two thousand years, plus.

Now, just in case I lost some of you in the process above, let me give clarification. I do believe that a three-and-a-half-year period will be occupied by the eighth beast's rule *(Revelation 13:5, Revelation 17)*. The book said so. However, I believe that the beast system will be a subtle destructive force for a period of forty-two measures — forty-two generations, or forty-two years, or forty-two months.

This subtle destructive force can be demonstrated as follows: Hypnosis, the demigod of sleep, is one of the marks of this "hour." Paul stated in *Romans 13:11* that "sleep" (Gk.; hypno) is also a spiritual state that was occurring in a time he called a "high time," which literally means an "hour." The word "dreamers" in Jude means that which is seen in sleep (Gk.; "in" plus "hupnos").

The world is in an hour of stupor; and they will be influenced mentally (marked) in a subtle manner. The mark, name and number of the beast is on the "hand" and "forehead" *(Revelation 13:16)*. "Forehead," in the Greek text, literally reads to change ("meta") eyes or sight ("ops"), or amidst ("meta") the eyes or sight.

The mark on the forehead points to someone's character of mind being changed by the "mark" (lit.; character) of the beast. One of the signs of this is the prevalence of unexplainable forgetfulness[11] in the land. People's minds are being influenced and taken by the spirit of the beast. The common expression of this is "I am having a senior moment." One of the definitions of "truth" means not to be unaware. Therefore, we must use the truth to fight the attitude of being mentally "unaware."

Also, if you can receive it, the beautiful worldly systems have been a subtle destructive influence since the reality of beast kingdoms was revealed by Daniel. Remember, Nebuchadnezzar (a policy maker) saw the kingdoms of the world as beautiful metals. However, a prophet, Daniel, saw the "truth" of the worldly kingdoms as "beasts" *(Daniel 2; Daniel 7)*. It is the same today.

---

[11] This statement is not referring to those who are carrying too much in their minds, and hence forget certain things instead of having a "To Do" list.

The beautiful dominions are but beast to God's prophets and apostles. The beast system is subtlety destroying civilization by its worldly attractions. (Remember Nebuchadnezzar also lost his memory in *Daniel, Chapter 2*.) Mankind is forgetting God as they are being made comatose by the beautiful beast system, and it is being done by an obtrusive evil.

Daniel 8:25, RSV: ... Without warning he shall destroy many ...

Daniel 8:25, NASU: ... And he will destroy many while they are at ease...

Daniel 8:25, KJV: ... and by peace shall destroy many...

Daniel 8:25, NKJV: ... He shall destroy many in their prosperity...

As stated above, I am not doing away with the forty-two months that were indicated in *Revelation 13:5*. I am merely showing what the duration of the "first hour" of the beast is relative to God's day year declaration in *2 Peter 3*. The hour can mean forty-two years, or it can mean forty-two generations of a two thousand year period, etc.

Every kingdom lasts for certain duration, and in that duration there are different leaders who rule that particular kingdom for a certain time. During a time of the forty-two years, the eighth beast will be manifested, whose deeds will intensify for a forty-two-month period; or during the forty-two generations of the beast rule, in the final days of the beast system.; as the Stone Kingdom[12] continues to cause the crumbling of the iron and the clay kingdom, it will be an intense divisive period in the earth.

---

[12] Please refer to the last chapter (The Lamb, The Only Potentate) of my book *The Lamb* for further development

Beastly mankind (6) will be against God and His Saints (7) —
6x7=42. God made Adam on the sixth (6th) day *(Genesis 1:26-31)*. The number of the beast "because of man" is "666"
(Revelation 13:18) Do you see it now?

During the period of the forty-two months, or the forty-two
generations, and/or the forty-two years, the beast will
intensify blasphemy[13] in the world through "the power of the
air" *(compare Ephesians 2:2; I Corinthians 14:9)*. The beast has
and will make intense war on the saints mentally, as indicated
earlier.

*Daniel 7:25, NKJV: He shall speak pompous words against the Most
High, Shall persecute ["but used only in a mental sense," Strong's
#1080 and 1086] the saints of the Most High, And shall intend to
change times and law. Then the saints shall be given into his hand
For a time and times and half a time.*

*Revelation 13:5-7, NKJV: [5]And he was given a mouth speaking
great things and blasphemies, and he was given authority to
continue for forty-two months (lit.; measures). [6]Then he opened his
mouth in blasphemy against God, to blaspheme His name, His
tabernacle, and those who dwell in heaven.[7]It was granted to him to
make war with the saints and to overcome them. And authority was
given him over every tribe, tongue, and nation.*

Before the kingdoms are "translated," there will be an hour
(the first hour) when a beast, its system and those who have
its mark, name and number will engage in intense war games
against the saints.

The phrase "he [the beast] was given authority to continue for
forty-two months," reads in the Majority Text as "he was
given authority to make war for forty-two months"

---

[13] The feet of the image seen by Nebuchadnezzar and interpreted by Daniel also
walked in "slander"

(Revelation 13:5). This makes sense in light of *Revelation 12:17,* "… and the dragon was enraged … and he went to make war with the rest of her offspring …."

The result of the dragon's determination was the beast rising out of the sea as a worshipped war monger *(Revelation 13:1-4)*. Thus, the beast's "war with the saints" *(Revelation 13:7)* is for forty-two months, literally, or it is for forty-two generations, by interpretation, and finally it includes forty-two years, by extension.

Whatever the duration is to you, make sure you keep on your helmet of the Defender (Jesus). The warfare will be mostly mental. The phrase, "Let this mind be in you which was also in Christ Jesus" has to do with Jesus' death on the cross *(Philippians 2:5-8)*.

Thus, the ability to embrace the cross was accomplished first in the "mind" of Jesus. There will be a spike in persecution against the saints during this "hour" of darkness. However, we have the mind of Christ which is to us a light; and we are victorious in any tribulations.

The Hour of the Dark Ones

Luke 22:52-53, NKJV: *52Then Jesus said unto the chief priests, and captains of the temple, and the elders, which were come to him, Be ye come out, as against a thief, with swords and staves?53 When I was daily with you in the temple, ye stretched forth no hands against me: but this is your hour, and the power of darkness.*

Jesus knew the hour of the dark one relative to His crucifixion. The highlighted phrase above literally reads: "this is the hour of you and the authority of the dark one."

Darkness is a noun, neuter, singular and is genitive in case. Therefore, it is not just the "hour ... of the authority of darkness;" but the "hour ... of the authority of the dark one." The writer personifies darkness (i.e., makes darkness a person).

Thus, the dark one is the source (genitive case) of the darkness. The "hour" also belongs to "the chief priests, and captains of the temple, and the elders" who crucified the Lord. Luke in reference to those who came to take Jesus quotes Him saying, "... this is your hour;" and, Jesus did not stop there. There is also an "hour ... of the authority of the dark one." What is this authority?

The authority to crucify the Son of Man! If you can receive it, it also points to the authority given to the dark ones to martyr some of the saints for approximately forty-two generations (one hour). No one could crucify Jesus until the authority was given. God gave the authority to the dark ones to be able to crucify Jesus to save us. The same is true for the generation of Christ.

John 19:9-11, NKJV: *10Then Pilate said to Him, "Are You not speaking to me? Do You not know that I have power to crucify You, and power to release You?" 11 Jesus answered, "You could have no power (lit.; authority) at all against Me unless it had been given you from above. Therefore, the one who delivered Me to you has the greater sin."*

Authority can only be given from "above." Therefore, God gave the release and the right "hour" to crucify the Son of Man. One of the root words for authority means "it is right," or "it is lawful." It was right for Jesus to die for us. God deemed it right, not man. According to *Romans, Chapter 5,* because sin and death passed down to us by one man, the gift of one man's (Jesus') "right act" causes us to reign in life through Jesus. Alleluia!

Remember in a previous chapter, I discussed the truth that "one hour" denotes approximately forty-two (42) years. I also indicated that this "forty-two years" also points to a generation called the forty-second generations. There is a forty second generation of the beast system, and there is a forty-second generation of Christ.

Allow me to develop the forty-second generation of Christ first, and then I will continue to discuss the hour (42nd generation) of the dark one.

Matthew 1:1, NKJV: The book of the genealogy of Jesus Christ, the Son of David, the Son of Abraham ....

Matthew 1:17, NKJV: So, all the generations from Abraham to David are fourteen generations, from David until the captivity in Babylon are fourteen generations, and from the captivity in Babylon until the Christ are fourteen generations.

The genealogy of Jesus from Abraham to Christ is forty-two generations (14 + 14 + 14=42). However, when the names are added there are only forty-one (41)[14] generations to Jesus *(Matthew 1:2-16)*. This is significant.

Let us do the count. Abraham (1), Isaac (2), Jacob (3), Judah (4), Perez (5), Hezron (6), Ram (7), Amminadab (8), Hahshon (9), Salmon (10), Boaz (11), Obed (12), Jesse (13), David (14), Solomon (15), Rehoboam (16), Abijah (17), Asa (18), Jehoshaphat (19), Joram (20), Uzziah (21), Jotham (22), Ahaz (23), Hezekiah (24), Manasseh (25), Amon (26), Josiah (27), Jeconiah (28), Shealtiel (29), Zerubbabel (30),Abiud (31), Eliakim (32), Azor (33), Zadok (34), Achim (35), Eliud (36), Eleazar (37), Matthan (38), Jacob (39), Joseph (40), Jesus (41).

As you can see, the total is forty-one (41), not forty-two (42), and there is a reason. In addition, before the forty-second generation is developed further, let us look at how David was a type of Jesus relative to the forty-first generation.

1 Samuel 17:15-20, NKJV: ¹⁵But David occasionally went and returned from Saul to feed his father's sheep at Bethlehem. ¹⁶And the Philistine [Goliath] drew near and presented himself forty days, morning, and evening. ¹⁷Then Jesse said to his son David, "Take now for your brothers an ephah of this dried grain and these ten loaves and run to your brothers at the camp. ¹⁸And carry these ten cheeses to the captain of their thousand, and see how your brothers fare, and bring back news of them." ¹⁹Now Saul and they and all the men of Israel were in the Valley of Elah, fighting with the Philistines. ²⁰ So David rose early in the morning, left the sheep with a keeper, and took the things and went as Jesse had commanded him. And he came to the camp as the army was going out to the fight and shouting for the battle.

Goliath tormented Israel for forty days. "Then" Jesse asked David to go and visit his brothers who were fighting for Saul.

---

[14] I heard this truth from Dr Turnel Joshua Nelson

The Scripture then indicated that David "rose early in the morning" — the morning after the fortieth day. Forty plus one equals forty-one (40 + 1=41).

It was on the forty-first day that David killed Goliath. This matches the forty-one generations until Jesus Christ. The application is: Goliath [Satan and/or demons mingled with humanity] tormented the people of the earth for forty generations. In the forty-first generation Jesus [the greater David] came and destroyed Goliath [Satan]. Do you see the correlation?

David, a type of Jesus, killed Goliath. He foreshadowed Jesus who destroyed the Devil single-handedly. This was done in the forty-first day or in the forty-first generation by Jesus Christ, Himself. What then does the phrase in *Matthew 1:17* really means: "So all the generations from Abraham to David are fourteen generations, from David until the captivity in Babylon are fourteen generations, and from the captivity in Babylon until the Christ are fourteen generations."

"Until the Christ" is the key phrase. Christ means Jesus and His Body (the Church). It did not say until Jesus. The writ says, "until the Christ." *Matthew 1:1* state "… the genealogy of Jesus Christ …" Matthew 1:17 says something entirely different. The end of the verse states "until the Christ."

1 Corinthians 12:12-13, NKJV: ¹²For as the body is one and has many members, but all the members of that one body, being many, are one body, so also is Christ. ¹³ For by one Spirit we were all baptized into one body — whether Jews or Greeks, whether slaves or free — and have all been made to drink into one Spirit.

Paul understood the meaning of baptism into one body. The entire Church is Christ — "all the members of that one body, being many are one body, so also is Christ." Do you see it? Therefore, the forty-second generation is the Christ — Jesus, the head of the Church, and His Body, the Church. This is why there are forty–one names, yet forty-two generations were numerated (14 +14+14=42).

The forty-second generation started in the days of John the Baptist and will continue until .... All who are sincerely baptized into the Body of Christ by the Spirit are the forty-second generation of Christ. Thus, all the Church with her many colored ethnicities is an hour-hand on God's clock.

In the Old Testament, whenever a man died without giving children to his wife, a next of kin was allowed to marry the woman to have children in the name of the dead husband *(see Ruth)*. Jesus ascended to heaven after His resurrection. The Holy Spirit is "another (Gk.; allos — another of the same kind) Helper" *(John 14:16)* was given as a Comforter in place of Jesus.

The union between the Holy Spirit and Jesus' Church will yield the same result as when the Holy Spirit gave Mary conception *(see Revelation 12)*. Another way of saying this is: by one Spirit, we are baptized into one body. In the same breath, Paul called this result of Spirit baptism into one body, Christ.

The forty-second generation is the Church becoming as Christ in one body with Jesus, who is the Christ. "Christ ...is the image of God" *(1 Corinthians 4:4)*. "He is the image of the invisible God" *(Colossians 1:25)*. And finally: "… we are … are being transformed into the same image..." *(2 Corinthians 2:18)*. Why is this forty-second generation so important?

There is and will be a generation who will be the living image of Jesus in every form; and one of the results of being like Jesus (i.e., walking in fruit and power) will be martyrdom. When God asked Abraham to offer up his son, God substituted Abraham's son with a ram whose "horns" were caught in the "thicket."

Genesis 22:13, NKJV: Then Abraham lifted his eyes and looked, and there behind him was a ram caught in a thicket by its horns. So, Abraham went and took the ram, and offered it up for a burnt offering instead of his son.

Revelation 5:6, NKJV: And I looked, and behold, in the midst of the throne and of the four living creatures, and in the midst of the elders, stood a Lamb as though it had been slain, having seven horns and seven eyes, which are the seven Spirits of God sent out into all the earth.

"Horn" in Scripture is symbolic of power. The Lamb has "seven horns" — power of the Holy Spirit without limit/measure. It was Jesus' spiritual power that really got Him in trouble; just like the ram's horns were the cause of the ram being sacrificed. The spiritual power of the Lamb of God was demonstrated when He raised Lazarus from the dead. The result was he got caught in the thicket by His horn. The Jews sought to kill him because of the resurrection power that flowed through Him.

John 11:43-53, NKJV: 43Now when He had said these things, He cried with a loud voice, "Lazarus, come forth!" 44 And he who had died came out bound hand and foot with grave clothes, and his face was wrapped with a cloth. Jesus said to them, "Loose him, and let him go ... 46But some of them went away to the Pharisees and told them the things Jesus did. 47Then the chief priests and the Pharisees gathered a council and said, "What shall we do? For this Man works many signs... 53 Then, from that day on, they plotted to put Him to death.

Why did they "plot" to put Him [Jesus] to death? Because He demonstrated the power of God by raising the dead! His "horn" of power got caught in the thickets of men's jealousy and insecurity. His power got Him in trouble.

The same thing happened to some who were part of the forty-second generation. Paul and Silas got whipped and put in jail for casting out a spirit of divination. They demonstrated power of the Spirit and got in trouble for it. They got caught in the "thicket" of man's abuse by their horn of power. Listen to the event.

Acts 16:16-24, NKJV: *[16]Now it happened, as we went to prayer, that a certain slave girl possessed with a spirit of divination met us, who brought her masters much profit by fortune-telling. [17]This girl followed Paul and us, and cried out, saying, "These men are the servants of the Most High God, who proclaim to us the way of salvation." [18]And this she did for many days. But Paul, greatly annoyed, turned and said to the spirit, "I command you in the name of Jesus Christ to come out of her." And he came out that very hour. [19]But when her masters saw that their hope of profit was gone, they seized Paul and Silas and dragged them into the marketplace to the authorities. [20]And they brought them to the magistrates, and said, "These men, being Jews, exceedingly trouble our city; [21]and they teach customs which are not lawful for us, being Romans, to receive or observe." [22]Then the multitude rose up together against them; and the magistrates tore off their clothes and commanded them to be beaten with rods. [23]And when they had laid many stripes on them, they threw them into prison, commanding the jailer to keep them securely. [24]Having received such a charge, he put them into the inner prison and fastened their feet in the stocks.*

The good thing about the outcome of Jesus and with Paul and Silas is: The same power that got them in trouble, the same power that delivered them. Jesus was raised from the dead by the power of God. Paul and Silas were delivered from the prison by the power of God. God sent an earthquake for Paul and Silas as they worshipped in their suffering.

There will be a forty-second generation who will become the image of Jesus and will flow in the power of the Spirit like Jesus. However, there will be a forty-second generation of the dark ones who will walk in the image of the beast; and they will kill some of the Church like the beast killed Jesus, Paul, Peter, Polycarp, the Christians in China during the Boxer Rebellion, etc. The key to this is that all things are done through God's permission. Remember "Job!" Satan could not touch "Job" until God permitted.

The "hour" of the dark one is the forty-second generation of the dark one who will kill the saints like they did Jesus. Martyrdom of some in the Church has been going on for millenniums. Forty-two (6 x 7=42), when looked at in a positive manner, is man with God (6 (the new man) times 7 (the number of God's rest)).

Conversely, forty-two (6 x 7=42) when looked at negatively, is man opposing God (6 — the beastly man) against 7 — the number of God's rest)). Did you catch it? In a season of the beast opposition against God, the dark one, in the person of the beast (its followers, and its system) will make war on the saints. Yet, that is not the end of the matter. The Lamb has and will overcome them, because "He is Lord of lords and King of kings" *(Revelation 17:14)*.

Revelation 17:14, NKJV: These will make war with the Lamb, and the Lamb will overcome them, for He is Lord of lords and King of kings; and those who are with Him are called, chosen, and faithful."

Beloved, the warfare is never one sided as some may think. The Church through the vessels that hold incense will judge the beast and its kingdom *(Revelation 16)*. The manifestation of persecution is a sign that the hour (generations) of the dark ones are ending. The very thing that the dark ones intended for evil against the Saints is the very thing that will destroy them.

The crucifixion of Jesus that Satan intended to completely destroy Jesus is the same "blood of His cross" that is used for the reconciliation of mankind with God. Something similar happened in the book of Esther, the tree that was intended to hang Mordecai is the same gallows tree on which wicked Haman was hung. There is an hour of the dark ones. However, there is simultaneously an hour (the forty-second generation of Christ) who executes God's judgment; and God's decision is always victorious for Himself and His Saints.

The Hour of His Crisis

Revelation 14:6-7, NKJV: ⁶Then I saw another angel flying in the midst of heaven, having the everlasting gospel to preach to those who dwell on the earth--to every nation, tribe, tongue, and people – ⁷saying with a loud voice, "Fear God and give glory to Him, for the hour of His judgment has come; and worship Him who made heaven and earth, the sea and springs of water."

Jesus is the criterion by which God judges; "because He has appointed a day on which He will judge the world in righteousness by the Man whom He has ordained" *(Acts 17:31)*. The hour of His judgment has come; and God is in a "crisis" for so the word "judgment" (Gk.; krisis) is transliterated from the Greek in the reference *(Revelation 14:7)* above.

Crisis means decisive moment, decision, distinct possibility of an undesirable outcome, etc. What is this hour of His crisis? I will develop this from four perspectives; and these perspectives are not exhaustive. As discussed earlier, an hour also points to the forty-second generation.

First, "the hour" of God's verdict has to do with a decision being passed by God on behalf of the forty-second generation of Christ. God will "give" judgment to the Saints of the Most High. The forty-second generation will recognize that they are indeed judges of the world and angels.

That is, the Church is also the "criterion" through which the world and angels are and will be judged. God's court will sit, and the court of God will pass judgment in favor of the Melchizedek Order. The Saints will "admit" the Kingdom of God into the earth with God as their Supreme Judge in His Supreme Court.

God is the "Judge" (Gk.; krites — noun, masculine, singular) of all *(Hebrews 12:23)*. There is also an "eternal judgment" *(Hebrews 6:2)*. "Judgment" in *Hebrews 6:2* is the Greek "krimatos," which is a noun, neuter in gender; and it is also genitive case.

"Krima" (the Greek for "judgment" in *Revelation 20:4)* is transliterated as "crime" in the English language; and a couple of the definitions of "krimatos" are one who judges a crime; one who brings a lawsuit; etc.

Thus, this eternal judgment has to do with Him, the Eternal Judge, whose verdict on crimes has an eternal effect. The Church is also given the ability to execute His eternal verdict. There is an eternal judgment in relation to the eternal gospel. In the words of Revelation, the hour of His verdict has come. Daniel teaches that God will be seated in His court as the Judge. He will "give" eternal authority of judgeship to His Saints.

Daniel 7:22, NKJV: Until the Ancient of Days came, and a judgment was made in favor (lit.; given to) of the saints of the Most High ...

Daniel 7:22, KJV: Until the Ancient of days came, and judgment was given to the saints of the most High ...

Revelation 20:4a, KJV: And I saw thrones, and they sat upon them, and judgment (Gk.; krima) was given unto them ...

Revelation 20:4a, NKJV: And I saw thrones, and they sat on them, and judgment was committed to them ...

Daniel 7:9-10, NKJV: [9]I watched till thrones were put in place, And the Ancient of Days was seated; His garment was white as snow, And the hair of His head was like pure wool. His throne was a fiery flame, Its wheels a burning fire; [10] A fiery stream issued And came forth from before Him. A thousand-thousand ministered[15] to Him; Ten thousand times ten thousand stood before Him. The court was seated, And the books were opened.

The *"court was seated"* and *"the Ancient of Days"* is the Judge. He will issue a ruling in favor of the Saints. God's decision will result in complete transfer of judgeship to the Saints (the forty-second generation of Christ), in lieu of the beast's system which is guilty of "crimes" against God and mankind. Some wrestle with how the kingdom of God's rule will be ushered in? The answer is simple.

God is going to pass a verdict through the court of His Church.; and the Scriptures indicate that the world's kingdoms will participate in allowing the Church's dominion to take the place of the kingdoms of the world.

God is the one who "gives" (appoints) rulers in the kingdom of men. However, in His hour of judgment, it is the Saints who will be "given" judgeship. Judgeship is a gift from God. Therefore, it is not of works; it is through faith.

Daniel 4:17, NKJV: This decision is by the decree of the watchers, and the sentence by the word of the holy ones, in order that the living may know that the Most High rules in the kingdom of men, gives it to whomever He will, and sets over it the lowest of men.

The Most High "gives" the kingdom of men to "whomever He will." It is that simple. Judgment was "given" to the "they" *(Revelation 20:4)*. The "they" that were "given" authority to judge are the "saints of the Most High" *(Daniel 7:22)*.

---

[15] A note for the Bible students: "ministered" is the Aramaic word "shemash" which corresponds to the Hebrew word "shemesh" ("sun")

Remember God is the Judge; and in the hour of His judgment, He "gives" the Church (those in whom Christ is formed) as the "criterion" of judgment. The criterion foremost is the measure of Jesus _in_ us. He is the judge in us and through us.

Acts 17:31, NKJV: Because He has appointed a day on which He will judge the world in righteousness by the Man whom He has ordained. He has given assurance of this to all by raising Him from the dead

He has appointed a day (1,000 years) when He will judge the world in righteousness "by the Man," Jesus. However, what are the mechanics of this "man." This "man" also points to the "one new man" Paul alluded to in *Ephesians 2:15.*

The "man" is that "perfect man ... the measure of the stature of the fullness of Christ" *(Ephesians 4:13b).* "We ... are being transformed into the same image" as Jesus *(see 2 Corinthians 3:18).* We are becoming like His "stature" (lit.; age).

There will be "One like the Son of Man" *(Daniel 7:13).* The more Jesus is "revealed" to us; the more we become "like Him" *(1 John 3:2).* God judges the world and angels by a "criterion." That criterion is the Church who has becomes the living "book" of Christ "known and read by all men." Our hearts are the open books on which the Holy Spirit writes the words of Christ.

Daniel 7:9-10, NKJV: ⁹"I watched till thrones were put in place, And the Ancient of Days was seated... The court was seated, And the books were opened.

2 Corinthians 3:2-3, NKJV: ²You are our epistle written in our hearts, known, and read by all men; 3 clearly you are an epistle of Christ, ministered by us, written not with ink but by the Spirit of the living God, not on tablets of stone but on tablets of flesh, that is, of the heart.

1 Corinthians 6:1-4, NKJV: ¹*Dare any of you, having a matter against another, go to law before the unrighteous, and not before the saints?* ²*Do you not know that the saints will judge the world? And if the world will be judged by you, are you unworthy to judge (Gk.; "kriterion") the smallest matters?* ³*Do you not know that we shall judge angels? How much more, things that pertain to this life?* ⁴ *If then you have judgments (lit; criteria) concerning things pertaining to this life, do you appoint those who are least esteemed by the church to judge?*

Paul considered the "criterion" of the Church to be the "valid" rule of law above the "opinion" of the beast's legal system—"… For out of Zion shall go forth the law … *(Isaiah 2:3)*. Paul called the courts of the beast system "least esteemed." Thus, the Christ-like generation who judges the world and angels are also the "criterion" of God.

The criterion is the "epistle of Christ" "known and read by all men" The Church is that entity called the "open books;" and the "criteria" for judgment are "written" in these books. The Church will "execute … the written judgment—this honor have all His saints" *(Psalm 149:9)*.

The second principle relative to God's hour of crisis is: there is a generation in His hour that will be affected by God's crisis—a decisive moment which is not necessarily desirable to God. Thus, it is also His crisis. The hour of God's crisis is also linked to humanity who dies without Christ.

Hebrews 9:27, NKJV: And as it is appointed for men to die once, but after this the judgment (Gk.; krisis) …

The statement above is a strong statement. Men are appointed to die. However, there is a judgment (crisis) after death. Most in the Christian world see this "judgment" in the future, and that is true but not complete. After a person dies, immediately, in the unseen that person is in a crisis. The

Scripture said, "... after this [death] the judgment (lit.; crisis) ..."

In other words, for those who are without Christ, and for those who faked their relationship with Jesus, there will be a crisis after they die and leave this world. Conversely, those who "hear" and "believe" in Him who sent Jesus "shall not come into judgment (lit.; crisis) but has passed from death into life" *(John 5:24).* At death there is a crisis for the unbelievers who do not heed the eternal gospel.

However, they are not the only one in crisis. God is also in a crisis at this hour, with regard to those who refuse to serve Him. There is a decision that He has to make reluctantly, after the death of some. He is not willing that any should perish, but that all should come to a place of changing their minds *(2 Peter 3:9; Revelation 16:9).*

Thus, in *Revelation 14:6-7* cited at the beginning of this chapter, He offered everyone the "everlasting" or (eternal) gospel." Why? He wanted to offer everyone eternal life because He is in the hour of His decision. It is an hour of crisis with respect to a decision He does not necessarily take pleasure in making. Let me say it another way. In this hour, the hour of His crisis, everyone who does not accept the eternal gospel is making an eternal decision. And for those who refuse the eternal gospel, there is a crisis they must face with respect to the person of Death *(Revelation 6:8)* and the reality of torment after death *(Luke 16:22-31),* with the understanding that God does not take pleasure in the death of the wicked *(Ezekiel 33:11).* When the wicked die without Jesus, it is an "undesirable outcome" for God. It is a crisis for the dead unbeliever; and it is crisis for God.

There is a day of judgment (crisis). Most think this day (1,000 years) is only future. Again, this is true but not complete. Judgment begins immediately after death, according to

Hebrews 9:27; and perfected love in us is the only fruit in us that will give us boldness. We get this boldness through the eternal gospel. Why do we need this boldness? It is the hour of God's crisis, and I believe that humanity who die without accepting the eternal One (Jesus) will be full of torment, of fear, after death.

1 John 4:17, NKJV: Love has been perfected among us in this: that we may have boldness in the day of judgment (Gk.; Krisis); because as He is, so are we in this world.

1 John 4:18-19, NKJV: 18There is no fear in love; but perfect love casts out fear, because fear involves torment (to dwarf, to curtail). But he who fears has not been made perfect in love. 19 We love Him because He first loved us.

Luke 16:22-23, NKJV: 22 ... The rich man also died ... 23And being in torments (or to go to the bottom) in Hades ...

"Boldness" in the Greek means "all out-spokenness," all rhetoric; therefore, when there is Love [Jesus] in us, in the day of crisis we can be out-spoken. Those who make Him Lord will not be tormented. Contrarily, those who refuse the eternal gospel in God's hour of decision are playing with fire, and when their crises come, they will not be able to say anything.

The torment of fear will be their crisis. Their rhetoric will not exist; because the One who is Love is not in their lives. What I am saying is: do not refuse the eternal gospel of the Merciful One. "Mercy triumphs (lit., boast) over judgment (lit.; crisis)" *(James 2:13b).* Do you see this?

Beloved we are in the hour (forty-second generation) of God's decision. We must heed the eternal gospel — "... fear God and give glory (lit.; good opinion) to Him ..." There are many who do not fear God; therefore, there is no change in their lives *(Psalms 55:19).* The Scripture states that the fear of the Lord is

75

to hate evil *(Proverbs 8:13)*. So, the angel was saying depart from evil because the hour of His decision has come. Humanity must also give Jesus "glory."

That is, we must maintain a "good opinion" (one of the literal meaning of glory) of the Father, the Son, and the Holy Spirit. The mind of the world and some Christians are filled with evil thinking about God. God is misunderstood by the majority, like the circumstances in the book of Job. The "everlasting gospel" is a gospel that preaches the fear of God and the glory (good opinion) of God.

Another aspect (a third principle) of the hour of God's decision concerns Babylon. The Scripture made an interesting statement. Her judgment happened in "one hour," or in the "first hour."

Revelation 18:10, NJKV: ... Alas, alas, that great city Babylon, that mighty city! For in one (or first) hour your judgment (Gk.; krisis) has come...

"Hour" denotes an hour, right time, fixed time, etcetera; therefore, in the right hour, in the "first hour," Babylon's crisis came. What is the hour "His of crisis or decision?" It is God's hour of decision to judge Babylon. Let me explain!

In Revelation 14:6-7, the everlasting gospel is offered in God's hour of crisis. In the following verse, *Revelation 14:8,* the next angel followed with words of judgment against Babylon. Babylon "is" fallen.

Revelation 14:8, NKJV: And another angel followed, saying, "Babylon is fallen, is fallen, that great city, because she has made all nations drink of the wine of the wrath of her fornication."

"Babylon is fallen, is fallen." Why? In one hour (the hour of God's crisis) her decision came. The decision to judge her — "for strong is the Lord God who judges her" *(Revelation 18:8 last part).* The angel declared Babylon "fallen" at the hour of His judgment, because she intoxicated all nations with her impure sexuality. One of the definitions for Babylon is confusion.

Everyone is confused concerning the right-sex and porno-sex (see my book *Sex-Pleasures* and my wife's book *Sexual Healing*). Babylon is a sexual addict. "She [Babylon] has made all nations drink of the wine of the wrath of her fornication (or lit.; porno)." Babylon is also the mother of porno *(Revelation 17)*. This means that whoever is caught up in her intoxication of her porno-sex will be confused about the rightness or wrongness of certain sexuality.

This is the hour when what is right in sexuality cannot be determined. There is so much mixture; confusion has set in. Thus, God must judge the entity that is propagating the wine of impure sex. For those who do not know, sexuality is spiritual.

What time is it? It is the hour of God's decision. He has to make some big decisions. He has decided to judge Babylon's sexuality. This will be done in the "first hour." The same "first hour" the beast will also be judged.

Sexuality in the world is in a crisis because God has placed His verdict on that arena. There is no fear of God in the land; and people are filling their lives with the toxicity of impure sex. The proof is in all the diseases that were developed in the body of most on the planet.

There are some Saints who are dealing with thing in their bodies that were inherited from Babylon before they became followers of Jesus. Why? In the world of Babylon, some received troublesome sicknesses[16] *(compare John 16:33, Revelation 16:2);* and God in His hour of decision determined Babylon to be judged. In fact, "in one hour her judgment has come" *(Revelation 18:10).* His purpose is to bring victory for His people. There is a call for God's people to get out of Babylon *(Revelation 18:4).*

Thus, the fourth facet of the "hour of His crisis" is that in His hour of crisis, God will "throw out" every crisis into victory on behalf of those who turn to Him. Matthew made an interesting observation in reference to Jesus' healing the multitude and Jesus remaining unseen, in the sense of not seeking prestige. He indicated that *"crisis"* will result in victory through the Lord on behalf of those who are narrowly hanging on.

Matthew 12:15-21, NKJV: *15But when Jesus knew it, He withdrew from there. And great multitudes followed Him, and He healed them all. 16 Yet He warned them not to make Him known, 17 that it might be fulfilled which was spoken by Isaiah the prophet, saying: 18 "Behold, My Servant whom I have chosen, My Beloved in whom My soul is well pleased! I will put My Spirit upon Him, And He will declare justice to the Gentiles. 19 He will not quarrel nor cry out, Nor will anyone hear His voice in the streets. 20 A bruised reed He will not break, And smoking flax He will not quench, Till He sends forth justice to victory; 21 And in His name Gentiles will trust."*

In other words, the hour of His crisis will also be distinguished by the victories that come out of His decision on behalf of Believers. The outcome for Him and his people may not appear as favorable decision; however, God has already won. He is always victorious in crisis. The Pharisees

---

[16] The Lord is the Healer of those who may have been affected by any diseases of Egypt (world) before they became followers of the Jesus. Be of good cheer, Jesus have overcome the world (Exodus 15:27; John 16:33; 1 Peter 1:24).

plotted against Jesus to kill Him because of His miraculous power that Jesus had demonstrated. He withdrew Himself.

The people wanted to spread His name abroad; He charged them not to do *(Matthew 12:10-21)*. Why? He would not defend himself with man's standard. In the words of Matthew, "He will not quarrel nor cry out..." It did not stop there. With respect to fame from men, Matthew said, "Nor will anyone hear His voice in the streets."

Today, there are a lot of ministers on the fame "kick." They want their "voices to be heard in the streets" of fame. However, they are not sending into victory the crisis that people are experiencing in their lives. Some are not really being delivered amidst the "hype" of today.

Jesus, in order to maintain His effectiveness, did not seek to be known for glamour. He would not allow praise of men and scare tactics of religious leaders to deter him. He remained meek and humble until victory was accomplished out of every crisis.

There are a lot of "Gentiles" who do not trust in His name" *(contrast Matthew 12:21)*. A couple of the reasons were cited above. Men want glory, and they defend themselves by man's standards. They quarrel over their doctrines, which brings me to a point: you can tell when a doctrine is not from God, men fight over it.

"Of these things put them in remembrance, charging them before the Lord that they strive (lit.; war) not about words (lit logos) to no profit, but to the subverting of the hearers" *(2 Timothy 2:14)*. However, God will have His victory out of the hour of His crisis. There are men and women who have a noble cause.

They will not quarrel about doctrines, and they will not look for fame by men, through men and for men *(Galatians 1:1)*. They will maintain a life of humility and meekness like Jesus, so that God may send forth all crises into victory. When it comes to the crisis of other people, it is not about us anymore. It must be about them. You will be victorious in every crisis.

In closing, God's hour of crisis consists of at least four outcomes. One, It is His decision that the Saints of the Most High become the judges of the world and angels. Two, it is an undesirable outcome (judgment) by God for people who die without accepting Jesus through the eternal gospel, because they have to face a crisis in the unseen hereafter.

Three, the sexuality of Babylon has been judged. The sexual arena of the world is under crisis. The outcome for Babylon is death, mourning, famine, and fire *(Revelation 18:8)*. The fourth, God will have victory in every crisis. People will be healed. He will not break those who are bruised; and He will not extinguish the fire of those who are about go out. In the hour of His crisis, God is victorious.

The hours are upon us, and the Wonderful One — Jesus — can tell us the ambient time. The last hour exemplified by the "Antichrist" and the "many antichrists" is happening before our very eyes. The overlap of the first hour discernible by the beast system with its mark on the forehead and hand (the way people think and use their hand to alter their very image internally and externally) are also before our very eyes. Yet, there is high expectation for the Church of Jesus.

Jesus also has His hour. The angel is still proclaiming "… fear God and give glory (lit.; good opinion) to Him, for the hour of His judgment has come." In His hour of crisis, I believe God will be victorious in every crisis. He will send every crisis into His victory. The forty-second generation of Christ through the Holy Spirit will "recognize" that the Church is indeed victorious in Jesus.

Matthew 12:20-21, NKJV: *20A bruised reed He will not break, and smoking flax He will not quench, till He sends forth justice (lit; crisis) to (lit.; into) victory; 21 And in His name Gentiles will trust.*

The name of the Lord Jesus Christ is glorified forevermore! Every hour of crisis will result in a victory for the Lamb of God and for the forty-second generation of Christ. We boldly declare His generation (Isaiah 53:8).

There is a generation — "One like the Son of Man" — who will reap the harvest for their Lord (The Lord of the harvest is Jesus) in this hour of decision, crisis, or turning point for all (Matthew 9:37-38; John 4:35-38; Joel 3:12-14; Revelation 14:14-20; Ephesians 4:13; Daniel 7:13-14; 1 John 3:2).

The grace of the Lord Jesus is with the spirits of those who belong to God by believing that Jesus is the Christ; and being filled with His Holy Spirit.

The Lord Jesus has come, He is coming, and He shall come!

Donald A. Peart

Other Books

Poiema, by Judith Peart
Wisdom from Above, by Judith Peart
Procreation, Understanding Sex, and Identity, by Judith Peart
100 Nevers, by Judith Peart
The Shattered and the Healing by Judith Peart
The Lamb, by Donald Peart
Jesus' Resurrection, Our Inheritance, by Donald Peart.
Sexuality, By Donald Peart
Forgiven 490 Times, by Donald Peart w/Judith Peart!
The Days of the Seventh Angel, By Donald Peart
The Torah (The Principle) of Giving, by Donald Peart
The Time Came, by Donald Peart
The Last Hour, the First Hour, the Forty-Second Generation, by Donald Peart
Vision Real, by Donald Peart
The False Prophet, Alias, Another Beast V1, by Donald Peart
"the beast," by Donald Peart
Son of Man Prophesy Against the false prophet, by Donald Peart
The Dragon's Tail, Prophets who Teaches Lies by Donald Peart
The Work of Lawlessness Revealed, by Donald Peart
When the Lord Made the Tempter, by Donald Peart
Examining Doctrine, Volume 1, by Donald Peart
Exousia, Your God Given Authority, by Donald Peart
The Numbers of God, by Donald Peart
The Completions of the Ages ... by Donald Peart
The Revelation of Jesus Christ, by Donald Peart
Jude—Translation and Commentary, by Donald Peart
Obtaining the Better Resurrection, by Donald Peart
Manifestations from Our Lord Jesus ...by Donald and Judith Peart).
Obtaining the Better Resurrection, by Donald Peart
The New Testament, Dr. Donald Peart Exegesis
The Spirit and Power of John, the Baptist by Dr. Donald Peart
The Shattered and the Healing by Judith Peart
Is She Married to a Husband? by Donald Peart
The Ugliest Man God Made by Donald Peart
Does Answering the Call of God Impact Your Children? by Donald Peart
Victory Out-of-the Beast-the Harvest of the Earth by Donald Peart
The Order of Melchizedek by Donald Peart
Ezekiel-the House-the City-the Land (Interpreting the Patterns)
Butter & Honey, Understanding how to Choose the Good and Refuse Evil, by Donald Peart

Contact Information:

Crown of Glory Ministries
P.O. Box 1041 Randallstown, MD 21133
donaldpeart7@gmail.com